ITALIAN COOKING

ITALIAN COOKING

General Editor: JENI WRIGHT

CONTENTS

General Editor: Jeni Wright
Consultant Editor: Giovanni Parmigiani
Authors:
Susanna Agnelli   Riccardo Di Corato   Maria Casati
Ilaria Rattazzi   Jeni Wright
Translator: Erica Propper

The recipes in this book are taken from
The Encyclopedia of Italian Cooking
first published in 1981 by
Octopus Books Limited

This edition first produced
exclusively for Tesco in 1984 by
Cathay Books Limited
59 Grosvenor Street, London W1

© Gruppo Editoriale Fabbri S. p. A., Milan
for the original Italian recipes

© 1984 Octopus Books Limited

ISBN 0 86178 266 6

Printed in Hong Kong

Introduction

The world-wide popularity of Italian cuisine is not surprising – it is basically simple, simply delicious, and many of the basic ingredients are now widely available. But there are different aspects to the cuisine, mainly due to historical and geographical influences. Italy is a country of regions (united in 1861) and two distinct areas: the north and the south. The more prosperous industrial north has the more fertile soil and here, flat pasta freshly made each day with eggs (pasta all'uovo), and butter are staples. In the south, manufactured tubular pastas are more popular, herbs and aromatics are much used and olive oil is the basic cooking fat.

The names of dishes vary from region to region, which can be confusing if you are not aware of the fact. For example, ravioli is also known as *tortellini, tortelli, cappelletti* etc. and pasta is called *tagliatelli, fettucine* and so on. In the following pages therefore, each recipe has the region of origin printed above the recipe title and in most cases an English title also. The exceptions are top favourites like *sabaione* which is not really translatable. But before you try some of the regional recipes, here are some notes on characteristics which they all share.

Herbs are probably the most important flavourings and, ideally, should be used fresh. If you have to use dried ones, be very sparing for they are much stronger. Basil (*basilico*), borage (*borago*), oregano (*origano*) and parsley (*prezzemolo*) are the four most used, particularly in salads, sauces, soups and pizzas. Bay leaves (*lauro*) are used in casseroles, soups, some roasts and baked fish dishes; sage (*salvia*) flavours liver and veal dishes; rosemary (*rosmarino*) is traditional with lamb, suckling pig, stews and soups – treat this herb with caution as it has a very distinctive flavour which, used indiscriminately, can be overwhelming.

Though herbs have largely replaced spices as flavourings, some spices are still commonly used: nutmeg (*noce moscata*) is the favourite for sweet and savoury dishes, and is always freshly ground; black pepper (*pepe*) is also ground fresh at the time of cooking or serving. Cinnamon (*canella*) is occasionally used in sweet dishes; coriander (*coriandolo*) seeds are crushed and added to meat dishes; saffron (*zafferano*) is prized for its colour in risottos, fish soups and stews; and crushed juniper berries (*ginepro*) are used to flavour pork, game and marinades. When salt is specified in a recipe, use coarse sea salt for the most authentic taste.

For flavouring purposes, the most important vegetables are fennel (*finocchio*); garlic (*aglio*) which is popular through-out the Mediterranean, not just Italy; and tomatoes (*pomadori*) – from the large, deep red marmande to the flavourful oval-shaped plum. In southern Italy especially, aubergines (*melanzane*), courgettes (*zuchini*), peppers (*peperoni*) and tomatoes – either fresh, canned or purée (paste) – are featured extensively.

Dried vegetables play an important role, too. Perhaps the most universal one is the strongly-flavoured dried mushroom (*porcini*), a little of which goes a long way. Pulses (*legumi secchi*) are also popular, the favourites being *borlotte* beans which vary in colour but are usually pinkish and speckled; the white *cannelini* and haricot (navy) beans; broad (*lima*) beans; chick peas (*ceci*), also called *garbanzos*; and lentils (*lenticchia*).

Sausages, cured meats and cheeses also figure largely in Italian cuisine and different types are produced in almost every region. For information on the main ones featured in the recipes, please refer to the Glossary on page 94.

The most widely used fat is olive oil (*olio*), though less expensive vegetable oils are available. The finest oil is said to come from Lucca in Tuscany and Trevi in Umbria. In northern Italy, butter is more popular simply because the cattle there produce sufficient milk for butter production. Around Rome, a mixture of half oil and half *strutto*, the Italian lard (shortening) is used; this has a neutral flavour and is excellent for roasts as well as for some cakes and pastries.

Small, elongated, creamy-white Pine kernels (*pinoli*) are much used in savoury as well as sweet dishes; it is difficult to find a satisfactory substitute for their distinctive flavour.

Vinegar (*aceto*) – always red or white wine vinegar, never the malt or distilled varieties – is used in salads and brushed on some meats, particularly game, before cooking.

Italy produces more wine than any other European country, and wine is an important cooking aid . . . when it should be the same quality as table wine; it is false economy to use a cheap wine which could ruin the dish. Barolo, Bardolino and Barbera are good red wines for table and pot; Soave, Frascati and Orvieto are respected whites. The fortified Sicilian wine, Marsala, is featured in much Italian cooking, both sweet and savoury, and there is no real substitute for this traditional ingredient.

North or south, while the ingredients vary, the exuberant attitude to cooking and eating does not: only the very freshest foods combined with perfectly complementary flavours will do.

Antipasti & Soups

Italians sometimes start their main meal of the day with an *antipasto*, which is a light starter or an appetizer rather than a substantial course.

Salami, cold meats and hams are very much a feature of *antipasti*. Sometimes a selection of different meats is served, but with *prosciutto di Parma* or *San Daniele*, the meat will normally be served on its own or at the most with melon or figs. *Bresàola*, a thinly sliced raw beef, is served with a very simple dressing of olive oil, lemon juice and pepper.

Fish is also served as an *antipasto*, particularly in coastal areas. Anchovies, sardines, whitebait, octopus and squid are served in numerous different ways: cold in an oil-based dressing, or fried and served hot with lemon.

Vegetables and salads make delicious light *antipasti*. Mushrooms, broad (lima) and French beans, courgettes (zucchini), artichokes, tomatoes, peppers, fennel and cauliflower are served raw or lightly cooked and chilled. They are generally tossed in a seasoned dressing of olive oil, garlic, lemon juice or vinegar, and freshly chopped herbs. *Cannellini*, haricot (navy) and *borlotti* beans are often served mixed with tuna fish and a garlic flavoured dressing.

Sometimes hot dishes are served as part of an *antipasto*. Bread is fried or baked with a topping like melted cheese or chicken livers and, in southern Italy individual pizzas, or *pizzette*, are a speciality.

The first course (*primo piatto*) is usually either a soup (*minestra*), or a consommé or clear broth (*brodo*), or a dish of pasta or rice. *Minestre* are usually substantial soups, with pasta or rice added; sometimes these are served as meals in themselves. *Minestrone* (see page 14) is a typical example of this kind of soup. Specific recipes are rarely followed – *minestre* are traditionally made with almost any ingredients that come to hand, including leftover meat and vegetables.

Brodo often have a little pasta, rice, toasted cheese or some croûtons added to them as they are not as substantial as *minestre*. *Zuppa* is another general Italian name for soup and *Zuppa alla pavese* (see page 12) is a well-known soup containing slices of bread topped with raw eggs. Fish soups or stews of the *bouillabaisse* type are usually called *zuppe di pesce*; they tend to be very substantial and are often meals in themselves.

It is customary to serve freshly grated Parmesan cheese with most Italian soups.

PIEMONTE & VALLE D'AOSTA

BAGNA CAÔDA

Anchovy Dip

Metric/Imperial	American
150 ml/¼ pint olive oil	⅔ cup olive oil
3 garlic cloves, peeled and crushed	3 garlic cloves, peeled and crushed
1 × 50 g/2 oz can anchovies, drained and roughly chopped	1 × 2 oz can anchovies, drained and roughly chopped
75 g/3 oz unsalted butter	⅓ cup sweet butter
bowl of sliced raw vegetables (eg. green peppers, carrots, turnip, celery, Jerusalem artichokes)	bowl of sliced raw vegetables (eg. green peppers, carrots, turnip, celery, Jerusalem artichokes)

Heat the oil in a small frying pan (skillet). Add the garlic and anchovies and simmer over low heat for 15 minutes, stirring occasionally. Add the butter and stir until melted.

To serve: stand the frying pan (skillet) over a fondue burner or spirit lamp at the table. Guests then dip the vegetables into the hot sauce.

SERVES 4 to 6

PIEMONTE & VALLE D'AOSTA

FONDUTA

Piedmontese Cheese Fondue

Metric/Imperial	American
300 ml/½ pint warm milk	1¼ cups warm milk
350 g/12 oz fontina cheese★, thinly sliced	¾ lb fontina cheese★, thinly sliced
pinch of salt	pinch of salt
4 egg yolks	4 egg yolks
50 g/2 oz butter, softened	¼ cup butter, softened
TO SERVE:	TO SERVE:
1 truffle or a few button mushrooms, thinly sliced	1 truffle or a few button mushrooms, thinly sliced
few slices toasted bread, cut into triangles	few slices toasted bread, cut into triangles

Set aside a few tablespoons of the milk. Pour the rest of the milk into a large heatproof bowl and stand over a large pan half-filled with gently simmering water. Add the cheese and salt and stir constantly with a wooden spoon until thick and smooth.

Mix together the egg yolks and the reserved warm milk, then stir into the melted mixture. Add the butter gradually, stirring until the fonduta becomes smooth and creamy.

Divide equally between small serving dishes (preferably earthenware). Spread the truffle or mushrooms on top. Serve immediately, with the toast.

SERVES 4 to 6

The history behind Piemonte's most original dish, *Bagna caôda*, is interesting. In the days when there was a heavy tax on salt, the Piedmontese used a lot of anchovies in their cooking – their natural saltiness was an easy means of avoiding tax.

ABOVE: **Fonduta; Bagna caôda**

TUSCANY

CROSTINI DI MILZA E FEGATINI

Chicken Livers on Fried Bread

Metric/Imperial	American
225 g/8 oz chicken livers	½ lb chicken livers
vegetable oil for shallow frying	vegetable oil for shallow frying
1 celery stick, minced	1 celery stalk, ground
½ onion, minced	½ onion, ground
4 tablespoons dry white wine	¼ cup dry white wine
salt and freshly ground black pepper	salt and freshly ground black pepper
1 tablespoon minced capers	1 tablespoon ground capers
1–2 tablespoons chicken stock (optional)	1–2 tablespoons chicken stock (optional)
6 slices stale bread, crusts removed, sliced	6 slices stale bread, crusts removed, sliced

Chop the chicken livers finely. Heat 1 tablespoon oil in a heavy pan, add the celery and onion and fry over gentle heat until lightly coloured. Add the chicken livers and fry for a further 5 minutes. Add the wine and continue cooking until it evaporates.

Add salt and pepper to taste, then the capers. Cook for a further 10 minutes, stirring frequently and moistening with a little stock if necessary. Remove from the heat, then purée in an electric blender or work through a sieve (strainer).

Heat the oil in a frying pan (skillet), add the slices of bread and fry until golden brown. Drain thoroughly. Spread thickly with the liver mixture and cut into triangles or fingers. Serve immediately.

SERVES 6

PIEMONTE & VALLE D'AOSTA

ZUPPA DI VALPELLINE

Cabbage and Cheese Soup

Metric/Imperial	American
1 Savoy cabbage	1 Savoy cabbage
12 slices toasted bread	12 slices toasted bread
100 g/4 oz bacon rashers, fried	¼ lb bacon slices, fried
250 g/9 oz fontina cheese★, sliced	9 oz fontina cheese★, sliced
pinch of ground cinnamon	pinch of ground cinnamon
freshly ground black pepper	freshly ground black pepper
1 litre/1¾ pints meat stock	4¼ cups meat stock
25 g/1 oz butter, diced	2 tablespoons butter, diced

Cook the cabbage in boiling water for 15 minutes, then drain thoroughly and separate the leaves.

Line the bottom of an ovenproof dish with 4 slices of toast. Cover with half the cabbage, bacon and cheese. Repeat these layers once more, then cover with the remaining 4 slices of toast. Add the cinnamon and pepper to taste to the stock then pour over the toast in the dish.

Bake in a preheated moderate oven (180°C/350°F/ Gas Mark 4) for 30 minutes. Remove from the oven, dot the butter over the top, then bake for a further 20 minutes. Serve hot.

SERVES 4 to 6

TUSCANY

ACQUACOTTA

Mushroom Savoury

Metric/Imperial	American
7 tablespoons olive oil	7 tablespoons olive oil
2 garlic cloves, peeled and sliced	2 garlic cloves, peeled and sliced
450 g/1 lb mushrooms, sliced	1 lb mushrooms, sliced
225 g/8 oz tomatoes, skinned and chopped	1 cup skinned and chopped tomatoes
450 ml/¾ pint light stock	2 cups light stock
salt and freshly ground black pepper	salt and freshly ground black pepper
6 large slices hot toasted bread, cut into quarters	6 large slices hot toasted bread, cut into quarters
65 g/2½ oz Parmesan cheese★, grated	½–¾ cup grated Parmesan cheese★
2 eggs, beaten	2 eggs, beaten

Heat the oil in a heavy pan, add the garlic and fry gently until browned. Add the mushrooms and cook for 5 minutes, stirring frequently. Add the tomatoes, stock and salt and pepper to taste. Bring to the boil, then lower the heat, cover and simmer gently for 15 minutes.

Divide the toast slices between individual dishes, then sprinkle with about half of the Parmesan. Mix the eggs with the remaining Parmesan and add to the mixture in the pan. Remove from the heat immediately and stir vigorously. Pour over the toast and serve immediately.

SERVES 6

FRIULI-VENEZIA GIULIA

PAPAROT

Spinach Savoury

Metric/Imperial	American
1 kg/2 lb fresh spinach	2 lb fresh spinach
150 g/5 oz butter	⅝ cup butter
3 garlic cloves, peeled and crushed	3 garlic cloves, peeled and crushed
65 g/2½ oz plain flour	⅔ cup all-purpose flour
salt and freshly ground black pepper	salt and freshly ground black pepper
little cornmeal	little cornmeal

Cook the spinach, with just the water clinging to the leaves after washing, until tender. Drain well, then purée in an electric blender or sieve (strain).

Melt the butter in a heavy pan, add the garlic and fry gently until browned. Remove the garlic from the pan, then stir in the plain (all-purpose) flour and cook for 5 minutes, stirring constantly.

Add the spinach and salt and pepper to taste and cook for a further 5 minutes. Stir in a little hot water and bring to the boil, then stir in enough cornmeal to make a fairly solid mixture. Cook gently for 30 minutes, stirring frequently. Serve hot.

SERVES 6

UMBRIA

LA CIPOLLATA

Onion Savoury

Metric/Imperial	American
750 g/1¾ lb onions, peeled and sliced	7 cups peeled and sliced onions
2 tablespoons olive oil	2 tablespoons olive oil
100 g/4 oz bacon, chopped	½ cup chopped bacon
few basil leaves, chopped	few basil leaves, chopped
salt and freshly ground black pepper	salt and freshly ground black pepper
350 g/12 oz tomatoes, skinned and mashed	1½ cups skinned and mashed tomatoes
3 eggs, beaten	3 eggs, beaten
75 g/3 oz Parmesan cheese★, grated	¾ cup grated Parmesan cheese★
4 slices hot toasted bread	4 slices hot toasted bread
few basil leaves to garnish	few basil leaves to garnish

Put the onions in a bowl, cover with cold water and leave to soak overnight.

Heat the oil in a large heavy pan, add the bacon and fry gently until browned. Drain the onions thoroughly, then add to the pan with the basil and salt and pepper to taste. Cook over low heat for 20 minutes, stirring occasionally.

Add the tomatoes, cover the pan, lower the heat and cook very gently for 10 minutes. Taste and adjust the seasoning. Beat the eggs and Parmesan together, then add to the soup. Remove from the heat immediately and stir vigorously. Put a slice of hot toast in each individual soup bowl, then pour over the hot soup. Serve immediately, garnished with basil.

SERVES 4

Savouries take their place as a first course in an Italian meal, quite the opposite of the British savoury which is traditionally served at the end. Italian savouries are usually made with fresh vegetables, and are invariably substantial. They should therefore be followed by a light main course.

MINESTRA DI RISO E RAPE

Rice and Turnip Soup

Metric/Imperial	American
400 g/14 oz white turnips, peeled and sliced	2¼ cups peeled and sliced white turnips
salt	salt
25 g/1 oz butter	2 tablespoons butter
1 small onion, peeled and chopped	1 small onion, peeled and chopped
75 g/3 oz bacon, chopped	⅓ cup chopped bacon
1.5 litres/2½ pints beef stock	6¼ cups beef stock
freshly ground black pepper	freshly ground black pepper
200 g/7 oz rice	1 cup rice
1 tablespoon chopped parsley	1 tablespoon chopped parsley
50 g/2 oz Parmesan cheese★, grated, to serve	½ cup grated Parmesan cheese★, to serve

Cook the turnips in boiling salted water for 15 minutes until almost tender; drain well.

Melt the butter in a pan, add the turnips and cook gently for 6 to 7 minutes, stirring occasionally. Meanwhile, put the onion and bacon in a separate pan and cook gently, stirring constantly, until lightly browned. Add the stock and salt and pepper to taste and bring to the boil. Add the rice, then lower the heat and simmer for 15 minutes until tender. Stir in the turnips and parsley, then remove from the heat. Serve hot, with Parmesan cheese handed separately.

SERVES 4 to 6

BRODO DI MANZO

Beef Consommé

This beef consommé is used as a basis for many soups, pasta, cheese and vegetables. It is also used as a stock for risottos and sauces.

Metric/Imperial	American
1 kg/2 lb lean beef, in one piece	2 lb lean beef, in one piece
1 onion, peeled	1 onion, peeled
½ stick celery	½ celery stalk
1.75 litres/3 pints water	7½ cups water
salt	salt

Place the beef in a large pan with the onion and celery. Pour in the water and season lightly with salt. Bring to the boil slowly and skim the surface. Cover and cook very gently for 5 to 6 hours; the soup should be just below simmering point.

Strain through a sieve (strainer) lined with muslin (cheese-cloth). Allow to cool, then remove the fat layer from the top. The consommé should be perfectly clear.

Serve hot or use as required for other dishes.

SERVES 4 to 6

ABOVE: **Minestra di gianchetti; Zuppa alla pavese; Minestra di riso e verze**

ZUPPA ALLA PAVESE

Consommé with Eggs

Metric/Imperial	American
100 g/4 oz butter	½ cup butter
8 small slices bread, crusts removed	8 small slices bread, crusts removed
4 eggs	4 eggs
75 g/3 oz Parmesan cheese★, grated	¾ cup grated Parmesan cheese★
1 litre/1¾ pints Brodo di manzo (see left)	4¼ cups Brodo di manzo (see left)

Melt the butter in a large frying pan (skillet), add the bread and fry until golden brown on both sides.

Put 2 slices of fried bread into each of 4 warmed individual soup bowls, then crack the eggs on top of the bread, taking care not to break the yolks. Sprinkle with the Parmesan. Bring the consommé to the boil, then slowly pour over the eggs. Serve immediately.

SERVES 4

MINESTRA DI RISO E VERZE

Cabbage, Rice and Bacon Soup

Metric/Imperial	American
25 g/1 oz butter	2 tablespoons butter
½ onion, chopped	½ onion, chopped
50 g/2 oz streaky bacon, chopped	¼ cup chopped bacon
400 g/14 oz cabbage, shredded	5¼ cups shredded cabbage
1.75 litres/3 pints Brodo di manzo (see opposite)	7½ cups Brodo di manzo (see opposite)
salt and freshly ground black pepper	salt and freshly ground black pepper
200 g/7 oz rice	1 cup rice
1 tablespoon chopped parsley	1 tablespoon chopped parsley
50 g/2 oz Parmesan cheese★, grated, to serve	½ cup grated Parmesan cheese★, to serve

Melt the butter in a large pan, add the onion and bacon and fry gently until lightly coloured. Add the cabbage and fry for 5 minutes, stirring frequently, then stir in the consommé. Bring to the boil, then add salt and pepper to taste. Lower the heat, cover the pan and cook gently for 30 minutes.

Stir in the rice and cook for a further 15 minutes or until tender. Add the parsley, then remove from the heat. Serve hot, with Parmesan cheese.

SERVES 4 to 6

MINESTRA MARICONDA

Beef Broth with Parmesan

Metric/Imperial	American
225 g/8 oz bread, crusts removed	½ lb bread, crusts removed
300 ml/½ pint milk	1¼ cups milk
100 g/4 oz butter	½ cup butter
4 eggs, beaten	4 eggs, beaten
150 g/5 oz Parmesan cheese★, grated	1¼ cups grated Parmesan cheese★
pinch of grated nutmeg	pinch of grated nutmeg
salt and freshly ground black pepper	salt and freshly ground black pepper
1.5 litres/2½ pints Brodo di manzo (see opposite)	6¼ cups Brodo di manzo (see opposite)

Crumble the bread into a bowl, add the milk and leave for 30 minutes.

Melt the butter in a small pan. Squeeze the bread as dry as possible, then add to the pan. Cook gently until dry but still soft, stirring constantly. Transfer to a bowl, then add the eggs, 100 g/4 oz/1 cup Parmesan, the nutmeg and salt and pepper to taste. Stir well to mix, cover and leave to stand for 1 hour.

Pour the consommé into a pan and bring to the boil. Stir in the bread mixture gradually, then simmer for 5 minutes. Serve hot, with the remaining Parmesan handed separately.

SERVES 4 to 6

It seems the Italians have an irresistible urge to cram their soups full of ingredients – it is even rare to find a clear soup without a little something floating in it. The history behind *Zuppa alla pavese* illustrates this point. The story goes that a Lombardian housewife gave this soup to Francis I after his defeat in the battle of Pavia in 1525. Thinking her plain broth too humble to give a king, and not hearty enough for a tired, hungry and dejected one at that, she quickly broke two eggs into it to make it more substantial.

MINESTRA DI GIANCHETTI

Whitebait Soup

Metric/Imperial	American
1 litre/1¾ pints fish stock	4¼ cups fish stock
350 g/12 oz fresh peas, shelled	2 cups shelled fresh peas
150 g/5 oz vermicelli or capelli d'angelo	5 oz vermicelli or capelli d'angelo
225 g/8 oz whitebait	½ lb whitebait
1 egg, beaten	1 egg, beaten
salt and freshly ground black pepper	salt and freshly ground black pepper

Pour the stock into a large pan and bring to the boil. Add the peas and simmer for 20 minutes. Add the vermicelli and whitebait and cook until almost tender. Stir in the egg and salt and pepper to taste; cook for 1 minute. Serve immediately.

SERVES 4

LOMBARDY

MINESTRONE ALLA MILANESE

Metric/Imperial	American
2 tablespoons olive oil	2 tablespoons olive oil
100 g/4 oz bacon, chopped	½ cup chopped bacon
1 onion, peeled and chopped	1 onion, peeled and chopped
1 garlic clove, peeled and chopped	1 garlic clove, peeled and chopped
225 g/8 oz tomatoes, skinned and chopped	1 cup skinned and chopped tomatoes
100 g/4 oz dried borlotti or red kidney beans, soaked in cold water overnight	⅓ cup dried borlotti or red kidney beans, soaked in cold water overnight
6 basil leaves, chopped	6 basil leaves, chopped
1 parsley sprig, chopped	1 parsley sprig, chopped
2 litres/3½ pints water	9 cups water
1 carrot, peeled and diced	1 carrot, peeled and diced
1 celery stick, diced	1 celery stalk, diced
275 g/10 oz potatoes, peeled and diced	2 cups diced raw potatoes
225 g/8 oz courgettes, diced	2 large zucchini, diced
225 g/8 oz cabbage, shredded	2¾ cups shredded cabbage
100 g/4 oz fresh peas, shelled	¾ cup shelled fresh peas
salt and freshly ground black pepper	salt and freshly ground black pepper
200 g/7 oz rice	1 cup rice
50 g/2 oz Parmesan cheese★, grated	½ cup grated Parmesan cheese★

Heat the oil in a large saucepan, add the bacon, onion and garlic and sauté for a few minutes. Add the tomatoes, beans, basil, parsley and water. Bring to the boil. Lower the heat, cover and simmer for about 1½ hours, stirring occasionally.

Add the carrot and celery and simmer for a further 30 minutes. Add the remaining ingredients, except the cheese, with salt and pepper to taste. Simmer for 20 minutes or until all the vegetables are tender.

Taste and adjust the seasoning. Leave the soup to stand for 5 minutes, then add the Parmesan. Serve hot.

SERVES 6

FRIULI-VENEZIA GIULIA

JOTA

Bean and Cabbage Soup

Metric/Imperial	American
400 g/14 oz dried haricot beans, soaked in lukewarm water overnight	2 cups dried navy beans, soaked in lukewarm water overnight
100 g/4 oz streaky bacon, chopped	½ cup chopped fatty bacon
2 small heads of cabbage, quartered	2 small heads of cabbage, quartered
2 tablespoons cumin seeds	2 tablespoons cumin seeds
1 bay leaf	1 bay leaf
salt	salt
4 tablespoons olive oil	¼ cup olive oil
2 garlic cloves, peeled and sliced	2 garlic cloves, peeled and sliced
2 tablespoons plain flour	2 tablespoons all-purpose flour
100 g/4 oz cornmeal	1 cup cornmeal

Place the beans and bacon in a saucepan and pour over water to cover. Bring to the boil, cover and cook for 1½ hours, adding more water as necessary.

Meanwhile put the cabbage in a separate pan with the cumin seeds, bay leaf, a little salt and a very little water and cook for 2 to 3 minutes, shaking the pan constantly.

Heat half the oil in another pan, add the garlic and fry until brown. Discard the garlic, then stir the plain (all-purpose) flour into the hot oil in the pan. Cook for 2 minutes, stirring constantly, then add the cabbage and cook for a further 5 minutes.

Transfer the cabbage to the pan containing the beans, add the remaining oil, then the cornmeal a little at a time, stirring well after each addition. Cook gently for 30 minutes, stirring frequently and adding more water or stock if too dry. Taste and add salt if necessary. Serve hot.

SERVES 4 to 6

The famous soup *Jota*, **from Friuli-Venezia Giulia, used to be regarded as a poor man's dish. The Triestines even had a saying about it: 'jota jota every day and never polenta and milk'. Nowadays they no longer feel this way about such a nourishing dish – it can be found on the menus of most fashionable restaurants in Trieste.**

ABOVE: **Jota; Minestrone alla milanese; Papazoi**

TRENTINO-ALTO ADIGE

ZUPPA DI ORZO

Barley Soup with Ham

Metric/Imperial

25 g/1 oz butter
1 onion, peeled and chopped
1 carrot, peeled and chopped
1 celery stick, chopped
100 g/4 oz raw ham or
    bacon, diced
250 g/9 oz pearl barley,
    soaked in cold water for 2
    hours
1·5 litres/2½ pints chicken
    stock
1 bay leaf
7 tablespoons single cream
40 g/1½ oz Parmesan
    cheese★, grated
salt and freshly ground
    black pepper

American

¼ cup butter
1 onion, peeled and chopped
1 carrot, peeled and chopped
1 celery stalk, chopped
¼ lb diced raw ham or
    bacon
1 cup pearl barley, soaked in
    cold water for 2 hours
6¼ cups chicken stock
1 bay leaf
7 tablespoons light cream
6 tablespoons grated
    Parmesan cheese★
salt and freshly ground
    black pepper

Melt the butter in a large pan, add the onion, carrot and celery and fry gently for 10 minutes. Stir in the ham, barley, stock and bay leaf. Cover and simmer very gently for 1½ hours, stirring frequently. Add the cream, Parmesan and salt and pepper to taste and stir well to combine. Serve hot.

SERVES 4

FRIULI-VENEZIA GIULIA

PAPAZOI

Sweetcorn, Barley and Bean Soup

Metric/Imperial

200 g/7 oz dried borlotti or
    haricot beans
200 g/7 oz pearl barley
100 g/4 oz fresh or frozen
    sweetcorn kernels
2 tablespoons olive oil
100 g/4 oz streaky bacon,
    finely chopped
2 garlic cloves, peeled and
    crushed
2 litres/3½ pints light stock
225 g/8 oz potatoes, peeled
    and diced
1 tablespoon chopped
    parsley
salt and freshly ground
    black pepper

American

1 cup dried borlotti or navy
    beans
1 cup pearl barley
¾ cup fresh or frozen kernel
    corn
2 tablespoons olive oil
½ cup finely chopped fatty
    bacon
2 garlic cloves, peeled and
    crushed
9 cups light stock
1½ cups diced raw potatoes
1 tablespoon chopped
    parsley
salt and freshly ground
    black pepper

Soak the beans, barley and fresh corn if using, in separate bowls of lukewarm water overnight.

Heat the oil in a large pan, add the bacon and garlic and fry until golden brown. Drain the vegetables and add to the pan with the stock. Bring to the boil, lower the heat and simmer for 45 minutes. Add the potatoes and cook for a further 40 minutes or until the vegetables are tender. Stir in the parsley and salt and pepper to taste. Serve immediately.

SERVES 6 to 8

Pasta

The exact origins of pasta making are not known, although records show that it was eaten in Roman times. Some believe that the Italians learnt the art of making pasta from the Chinese, when Marco Polo returned to Italy from the East in the thirteenth century, but there are few Italians who would agree with this theory.

The history of pasta eating in Italy has been the subject of a great debate, but historical records show that the ancient Romans ate pasta as long ago as the 4th or 5th centuries BC, and therefore most people believe that the Etruscans introduced pasta into Italy. The exact nutritional value of commercial pasta varies, but most good quality brands contain as much as 13 per cent protein as well as vitamins, minerals and a small amount of fat. Although pasta is high in carbohydrate, it is usually the sauce served with it that is more fattening than the pasta itself.

The finest commercial pasta is made of durum wheat, mostly imported from Canada. When buying commercial pasta it is wise to read the label on the packet to ensure that this kind of wheat has been used. Durum wheat is one of the hardest varieties of wheat, and when making pasta only the endosperm of the grain kernel is milled into semolina, which is then mixed with water to make the dough. Dried pasta, like spaghetti and other tubular varieties, is more common in southern Italy and abroad than it is in the north of Italy, where the pasta is more likely to be the flat kind, often made with fresh eggs.

Making Pasta

Making pasta at home is not a difficult task, especially if you are used to pastry making, since the skills are similar. It is well worth the effort of mastering the art of pasta making, because the dried varieties, although convenient, cannot compare in flavour to homemade pasta, which is also much lighter in texture. There are no special secrets to pasta making, but once the dough is mixed it should be kneaded thoroughly until very, very smooth, elastic and free from lumps. To prevent the dough from drying out and cracking after kneading and before rolling, it should be wrapped in a cloth wrung out in warm water, then left to rest for about 10 minutes. Rolling and stretching the dough requires the most time, and this is where most cooks cannot spare the patience and energy, for the dough should be so paper-thin that it is almost possible to see through it. It must be dusted frequently with flour throughout this process, as it tends to become sticky with constant handling, and you will need a very large pastry board, table or work surface to allow yourself room to work. (Dividing the dough into two also makes this easier.)

Cutting pasta

The easiest kind of pasta to make at home is the ribbon noodle type known as *tagliatelle* or *fettuccine*, since this can be cut into thin strips simply with a sharp knife. There are various pasta cutting gadgets available from specialist kitchenware shops, the most common ones being noodle machines with which the dough can be rolled and cut by the simple turning of a handle. There are also round and square ravioli cutters, and ravioli trays which have wells with sharp edges – the dough is rolled over the tray with a rolling pin and the shapes are cut out automatically. After cutting the dough, it should be left for about 10 minutes to dry out before cooking.

PASTA ALL'UOVO
Plain Egg Pasta

Metric/Imperial	American
225 g/8 oz plain flour	*2 cups all-purpose flour*
2 large eggs	*2 eggs*
2 teaspoons oil	*2 teaspoons oil*
½ teaspoon salt	*½ teaspoon salt*
a little water	*a little water*

Sift the flour onto a work surface and make a well in the centre. Put the eggs, oil and salt into the well and mix together with the fingertips. Gradually draw the flour into the egg mixture and knead together, adding a little water if the dough seems dry. Dust the work surface with flour and knead the dough firmly until smooth and elastic. Wrap in cling film (plastic wrap) and set aside for about 1 hour.

Roll out the dough on a lightly floured surface, first in one direction and then the other, until it is paper-thin. Dust lightly with flour and leave to rest for 10 to 20 minutes to allow the pasta to dry slightly. It is then ready to be cut into the required shapes.

After cutting the dough leave it for about 10 minutes to dry out before cooking.

MAKES ABOUT 350 g/12 OZ PASTA

Pasta verde

Pasta verde is *pasta all'uovo* coloured green with spinach. It is an attractive pale green colour flecked with darker green. Use the basic recipe above and add 50 g/2 oz/¼ cup cooked spinach (squeezed very dry and either sieved (strained) or chopped very finely) with the eggs. Follow the recipe as above, remembering that this pasta is stickier than plain pasta and it will be necessary to flour the work surface more frequently.

MAKES ABOUT 400 g/14 OZ PASTA

Cannelloni: Cut the pasta into rectangles, about 7.5 × 10 cm/3 × 4 inches.

Lasagne: Either cut into strips, about 1 cm/½ inch wide, or into rectangles 7.5 × 13 cm/3 × 5 inches.

Taliarini, tagliatelle or fettuccine: Roll the sheet of pasta loosely into a Swiss (jelly) roll shape, and with a sharp knife cut across into even strips 3 mm/⅛ inch wide for *taliarini*, 5 mm/¼ inch for *tagliatelle* or *fettuccine*. Shake out the strips lightly so that they unroll, and leave to dry.

RAVIOLI GENOVESE

Metric/Imperial	American
FILLING:	FILLING:
25 g/1 oz butter	2 tablespoons butter
3 tablespoons olive oil	3 tablespoons olive oil
1 onion, peeled and finely chopped	1 onion, peeled and finely chopped
1 celery stick, finely chopped	1 celery stalk, finely chopped
1 small carrot, peeled and finely chopped	1 small carrot, peeled and finely chopped
1 bay leaf	½ bay leaf
1 clove	1 clove
225 g/8 oz piece stewing beef	½ lb piece stewing beef
salt and freshly ground black pepper	salt and freshly ground black pepper
3–4 tablespoons white wine	3–4 tablespoons white wine
1 tablespoon tomato purée	1 tablespoon tomato paste
75 g/3 oz Parmesan cheese★, grated	¾ cup grated Parmesan cheese★
2 eggs, beaten	2 eggs, beaten
pinch of grated nutmeg	pinch of grated nutmeg
175 g/6 oz fresh breadcrumbs (approximately)	3 cups fresh bread crumbs (approximately)
PASTA:	PASTA:
450 g/1 lb pasta all'uovo (see page 16: 1½ × quantity)	1 lb pasta all'uovo (see page 16: 1½ × quantity)
TO FINISH:	TO FINISH:
1.5 litres/2½ pints beef stock	6¼ cups beef stock
50 g/2 oz Parmesan cheese★, grated	¼ cup grated Parmesan cheese★

To make the filling: heat the butter and oil in a heavy pan, add the onion and fry gently until golden. Add the celery, carrot, bay leaf and clove and cook gently for 5 minutes. Add the beef and salt and pepper to taste and fry until golden brown on all sides. Add the wine, boil until it evaporates, then add the tomato purée (paste) dissolved in a little warm water. Cover the pan and simmer for 2 hours.

Meanwhile make the pasta and leave to stand for 1 hour.

Remove the meat from the pan and mince (grind) it into a bowl. Remove the clove and bay leaf from the cooking liquor, then add the liquor to the meat with the Parmesan, 1 beaten egg and the nutmeg. Stir in enough breadcrumbs to bind the mixture.

Divide the dough in half and roll each piece into a paper-thin sheet. Put heaped teaspoonfuls of the filling at regular intervals, about 5 cm/2 inches apart on one piece of dough. Brush the other sheet of dough with the remaining beaten egg and place loosely over the filling. Press the pasta between the filling firmly to seal. Cut around the balls of filling with a rotary cutter, then place the ravioli on a cloth sprinkled with flour.

Bring the stock to the boil in a large pan. Add the ravioli and cook for 5 minutes or until they rise to the surface. Transfer to a warmed serving dish with a slotted spoon. Add the Parmesan and fold gently to mix. Serve immediately.

SERVES 6

COLZETTI ALLA POLCEVERASCA

Pasta Shapes with Butter and Marjoram

If pine kernels are not available, use chopped walnuts instead.

Metric/Imperial	American
PASTA:	PASTA:
350 g/12 oz pasta all'uovo (see page 16)	¾ lb pasta all'uovo (see page 16)
TO SERVE:	TO SERVE:
75 g/3 oz butter	6 tablespoons butter
1 tablespoon chopped pine kernels	1 tablespoon chopped pine kernels
1 tablespoon chopped marjoram	1 tablespoon chopped marjoram
75 g/3 oz Parmesan cheese★, grated	¾ cup grated Parmesan cheese★

Make the pasta and leave to stand for 1 hour.

Knead the dough well, then divide into small balls about the size of walnuts. Flatten the balls of dough with the fingertips dipped in flour, then form each one into a figure-of-eight shape. Place the shapes on a cloth sprinkled with flour and leave to dry in a cool place for 1 hour.

Cook the pasta shapes in plenty of boiling salted water for 5 minutes or until they rise to the surface. Remove from the pan with a slotted spoon as soon as they are cooked and pile into a warmed serving dish; keep hot.

Melt the butter in a small pan, add the pine kernels and marjoram and heat, stirring, for 1 minute, then pour over the colzetti. Sprinkle with the Parmesan and serve immediately.

SERVES 4

During the 'pasta war' in the Italian press in the 1930s, journalists, cooks, restaurant owners and even doctors attacked each other over the subject of pasta. One poet even went as far as to say that pasta was 'an obsolete heavy food, inducing scepticism, sloth and pessimism'.

EMILIA-ROMAGNA

CAPPELLETTI DI MAGRO

Ravioli with Cheese Filling

In Emilia-Romagna and most of the nothern regions of Italy, pasta is usually made at home. Eggs are nearly always included in the dough and the finished pasta is served with a substantial filling or sauce. The dishes on these and the following two pages are typical of the area.

Metric/Imperial

PASTA:
400 g/14 oz plain flour
salt
4 eggs, beaten
FILLING:
225 g/8 oz ricotta cheese★
100 g/4 oz Bel Paese
cheese★, grated
50 g/2 oz Parmesan
cheese★, grated
2 eggs, beaten
pinch of grated nutmeg
TO SERVE:
1.5 litres/2½ pints stock or
water
100 g/4 oz butter, melted
75 g/3 oz Parmesan
cheese★, grated

American

PASTA:
3½ cups all-purpose flour
salt
4 eggs, beaten
FILLING:
1 cup ricotta cheese★
½ cup grated Bel Paese
cheese★
½ cup grated Parmesan
cheese★
2 eggs, beaten
pinch of grated nutmeg
TO SERVE:
6¼ cups stock or water
½ cup butter, melted
¾ cup grated Parmesan
cheese★

To make the pasta: sift the flour and a pinch of salt onto a work surface and make a well in the centre. Add the eggs and mix to a smooth dough. Shape into a ball, wrap in a damp cloth and leave to stand for about 30 minutes.

Meanwhile, make the filling: put the ricotta and Bel Paese in a bowl and beat well. Add the Parmesan, eggs, a pinch of salt and the nutmeg and beat thoroughly.

Roll out the dough to a paper-thin sheet. Cut into 4 cm/1¾ inch squares with a tooth-edged rotary cutter. Put a little filling in the centre of each square, then fold the dough over the filling to make triangles. Turn the corners of the triangles upwards.

Bring the stock or salted water to the boil in a large pan. Add the ravioli and cook for 5 minutes or until they rise to the surface. Remove from the pan with a slotted spoon and pile into a warmed serving dish. Sprinkle the melted butter and Parmesan over the top and serve immediately.

SERVES 4

GARGANELLI DI LUGO

Macaroni with Meat and Vegetable Ragù

Metric/Imperial	American
PASTA:	PASTA:
400 g/14 oz plain flour	3½ cups all-purpose flour
pinch of salt	pinch of salt
4 eggs, beaten	4 eggs, beaten
25 g/1 oz Parmesan cheese★, grated	¼ cup grated Parmesan cheese★
pinch of grated nutmeg	pinch of grated nutmeg
RAGÙ:	RAGÙ:
25 g/1 oz mushrooms	¼ cup mushrooms
1 onion, peeled	1 onion, peeled
1 carrot, peeled	1 carrot, peeled
1 celery stick	1 celery stalk
50 g/2 oz raw ham or bacon	1 thick slice raw ham or bacon
65 g/2½ oz butter	5 tablespoons butter
4 tablespoons olive oil	¼ cup olive oil
¼ cup grated Parmesan	⅔ cup beef stock
¼ pint/150 ml beef stock	⅓ cup ground beef
75 g/3 oz minced beef	⅓ cup ground pork
75 g/3 oz minced pork	7 tablespoons red wine
7 tablespoons red wine	1¾ cups skinned and mashed tomatoes
400 g/14 oz tomatoes, skinned and mashed	salt and freshly ground black pepper
salt and freshly ground black pepper	1 cup frozen peas
100 g/4 oz frozen peas	¾ cup grated Parmesan cheese★, to serve
75 g/3 oz Parmesan cheese★, grated, to serve	

To make the pasta: sift the flour and salt onto a work surface, then make a well in the centre. Add the eggs, Parmesan and nutmeg and mix to a smooth dough. Leave to stand for 20 minutes.

Flatten the dough with a rolling pin and roll into a sheet that is not too thin. Cut into 2 cm/¾ inch squares. Roll each square, corner to corner, round the handle of a wooden spoon to form macaroni.

To make the ragù: mince (grind) the mushrooms with the onion, carrot, celery and ham or bacon. Heat 50 g/2 oz/¼ cup butter and the oil in a heavy pan, add the minced (ground) mixture and simmer for 10 minutes, adding the stock gradually during cooking.

Add the minced (ground) meats and cook over a high heat for 5 minutes. Stir in the wine, cover and simmer very gently for 15 minutes.

Add the tomatoes, a little more stock and salt and pepper to taste. Cover again and cook for a further 30 minutes, adding more stock if necessary.

Melt the remaining butter in a separate pan, add the peas and cook for 5 minutes. Stir into the ragù and cook for a further 5 minutes.

Cook the macaroni in plenty of boiling salted water until al dente. Drain thoroughly and pile into a warmed serving dish. Top with the ragù and Parmesan. Serve immediately.

SERVES 4

ABOVE: **Preparing Cappelleti di magro and Gnocco fritto**

GNOCCO FRITTO

Fried Pasta Shapes

Metric/Imperial	American
350 g/12 oz plain flour	3 cups all-purpose flour
pinch of salt	pinch of salt
40 g/1½ oz lard	3 tablespoons shortening
vegetable oil for shallow-frying	vegetable oil for shallow-frying

Sift the flour and salt onto a work surface and make a well in the centre. Add the lard (shortening) and mix together with enough lukewarm water to give a smooth dough. Knead well until no longer sticky, adding a little extra flour if necessary. Flatten the dough with a rolling pin and roll out to a thin sheet. Cut into rectangular shapes, about 7.5 × 3 cm/3 × 1½ inches and prick all over with a fork.

Shallow-fry the rectangles a few at a time in hot oil until golden brown. Drain on absorbent kitchen paper while frying the remainder. Serve hot with an assortment of sausages.

SERVES 4

CANNELLONI PIACENTINI

Cannelloni Piacenza Style

Metric/Imperial	American
PASTA:	PASTA:
200 g/7 oz plain flour	1¾ cups all-purpose flour
salt	salt
2 eggs, beaten	2 eggs, beaten
2 egg yolks	2 egg yolks
50 g/2 oz butter, melted	¼ cup butter, melted
300 ml/½ pint milk (approximately)	1¼ cups milk (approximately)
FILLING:	FILLING:
900 g/2 lb fresh spinach, cooked, well drained and chopped	2 lb fresh spinach, cooked, well drained and chopped
1 tablespoon chopped parsley	1 tablespoon chopped parsley
150 g/5 oz ricotta cheese★	⅔ cup ricotta cheese★
100 g/4 oz mascarpone cheese★	½ cup mascarpone cheese★
65 g/2½ oz Parmesan cheese★, grated	⅔ cup grated Parmesan cheese★
1 egg, beaten	1 egg, beaten
1 egg yolk	1 egg yolk
pinch of grated nutmeg	pinch of grated nutmeg
TO FINISH:	TO FINISH:
50 g/2 oz Parmesan cheese★, grated	½ cup grated Parmesan cheese★
75 g/3 oz butter, melted	⅓ cup butter, melted

To make the pasta: sift the flour and a pinch of salt into a bowl. Add the eggs, egg yolks and 1 tablespoon melted butter, then stir in the milk gradually, adding enough to give a semi-liquid batter. Continue stirring for a further 10 minutes.

Heat 1 tablespoon of the remaining butter in a small frying pan (skillet). Pour in just enough batter to cover the bottom, tilting the pan to spread evenly. Fry until golden on both sides. Remove from the pan and repeat with the remaining batter, adding more butter to the pan as necessary. Trim the fritters to a rectangular shape.

To make the filling: put the spinach, parsley and ricotta in a bowl and beat well. Add the mascarpone, Parmesan, egg, egg yolk, nutmeg and a pinch of salt. Stir well. Divide the filling between the pasta rectangles, placing it in the centre of each one. Fold the edges over the filling, to form a parcel shape.

Arrange the cannelloni in a single layer in a buttered ovenproof dish. Sprinkle with the Parmesan and the butter and bake in a preheated moderately hot oven (200°C/400°F/Gas Mark 6) for 20 minutes until golden brown. Serve hot.

SERVES 4

BELOW: **Cannelloni piacentini; Lasagne alla bolognese**

CRESCENTINE
Tuscan Deep-Fried Pasta

Metric/Imperial	American
½ teaspoon dried yeast	½ teaspoon active dry yeast
¼ teaspoon sugar	¼ teaspoon sugar
450 g/1 lb plain flour	4 cups all-purpose flour
salt	salt
25 g/1 oz butter	2 tablespoons butter
150 ml/¼ pint lukewarm stock	⅔ cup lukewarm stock
vegetable oil for deep-frying	vegetable oil for deep-frying
freshly ground black pepper	freshly ground black pepper

Dissolve the yeast and sugar in a little water; set aside for 10 minutes. Sift the flour and a little salt onto a work surface. Stir in the yeast, then add the butter and enough stock to make a soft dough. Knead well, then roll out to a fairly thick sheet.

Fold the 4 corners of the dough inwards to the centre, then flatten with the rolling pin. Fold and flatten again at least 5 more times. Roll the dough out to a sheet, about 5 mm/¼ inch thick, and cut into small rectangles.

Deep-fry the shapes, a few at a time, in hot oil until golden brown and puffed up. Drain on absorbent kitchen paper while frying the remainder. Sprinkle with salt and pepper and serve hot.

SERVES 6

In the north of Italy, cannelloni is most frequently made at home by wrapping rectangular pieces of dough around a filling. Southern Italians are more likely to use packets of ready-made tubes when making cannelloni.

LASAGNE ALLA BOLOGNESE

Metric/Imperial	American
225 g/8 oz green or plain lasagne	½ lb green or plain lasagne
RAGÙ:	RAGÙ:
15 g/½ oz butter	1 tablespoon butter
1 onion, peeled and finely chopped	1 onion, peeled and finely chopped
1 small carrot, peeled and finely chopped	1 small carrot, peeled and finely chopped
1 celery stick, finely chopped	1 celery stalk, finely chopped
3 rashers bacon, finely chopped	3 bacon slices, finely chopped
350 g/12 oz finely minced beef	1½ cups finely ground beef
100 g/4 oz chicken livers, finely minced	¼ lb chicken livers, finely chopped
4 tablespoons dry white wine	4 tablespoons dry white wine
300 ml/½ pint beef stock	1¼ cups beef stock
1 tablespoon tomato purée	1 tablespoon tomato paste
grated nutmeg	grated nutmeg
salt and freshly ground black pepper	salt and freshly ground black pepper
BÉCHAMEL SAUCE:	BÉCHAMEL SAUCE:
40 g/1½ oz butter	3 tablespoons butter
40 g/1½ oz plain flour	⅓ cup all-purpose flour
600 ml/1 pint warm milk	2½ cups warm milk
4 tablespoons double cream	¼ cup heavy cream
grated nutmeg	grated nutmeg
50 g/2 oz Parmesan cheese★, grated	½ cup grated Parmesan cheese★

To make the ragù: melt the butter in a large shallow pan. Add the vegetables and bacon and fry gently, stirring, for about 10 minutes until golden. Add the beef and fry, stirring, until evenly browned. Add the chicken livers and cook, stirring, for 1 to 2 minutes, then add the wine, stock, tomato purée (paste), nutmeg and salt and pepper to taste. Bring to the boil, cover and simmer gently for 1 hour, stirring occasionally.

Cook the lasagne in a large pan of boiling salted water until al dente, stirring occasionally to prevent the pasta sticking. Immediately add cold water to the pan to prevent further cooking, drain and lay the strips side by side on a clean tea towel.

To make the Béchamel sauce: melt the butter in a pan, stir in the flour and cook for 1 minute. Take off the heat and stir in the milk and cream. Return to the heat and cook, stirring, until smooth. Season with salt and nutmeg to taste. Put a layer of lasagne in the bottom of a buttered ovenproof dish. Cover with a layer of ragù, then a layer of béchamel and sprinkle with a little Parmesan. Continue these layers, finishing with a thick layer of Béchamel sauce and a good sprinkling of Parmesan. Bake in a preheated moderately hot oven (200°C/400°F/Gas Mark 6) for 30 minutes, or until golden on top. Serve immediately.

SERVES 6

MACCHERONI ALLA PESARESE

Zitone Pesaro Style

Metric/Imperial	American
175 g/6 oz turkey breast meat	6 oz turkey breast meat
2 chicken livers	2 chicken livers
100 g/4 oz ham	¼ lb ham
50 g/2 oz mushrooms	½ cup mushrooms
100 g/4 oz butter	½ cup butter
1 small onion, peeled and chopped	1 small onion, peeled and chopped
7 tablespoons dry white wine	7 tablespoons dry white wine
pinch of grated nutmeg	pinch of grated nutmeg
salt and freshly ground black pepper	salt and freshly ground black pepper
7 tablespoons cream	7 tablespoons cream
300 g/11 oz zitone	11 oz zitone
75 g/3 oz gruyère cheese, grated	¾ cup grated gruyère cheese

Mince (grind) the turkey, chicken livers, ham and mushrooms. Melt 2 tablespoons butter in a heavy pan, add the onion and fry gently until golden. Stir in the minced (ground) mixture and cook, stirring, for 10 minutes.

Add the wine and simmer gently until it has evaporated by half, then add the nutmeg and salt and pepper to taste. Transfer to a bowl, add a little of the cream and stir well, to give a smooth, creamy filling.

Cook the zitone in plenty of boiling salted water until *al dente*. Drain thoroughly, then stuff with the filling.

Arrange the stuffed zitone in two layers in a buttered baking dish, covering each layer with the cream and gruyère. Dot the remaining butter over the top. Bake in a preheated moderately hot oven (200°C/400°F/Gas Mark 6) for 15 minutes. Serve hot.

SERVES 4

SPAGHETTI CACIO E PEPE

Spaghetti with Pecorino Cheese

Metric/Imperial	American
400 g/14 oz spaghetti	14 oz spaghetti
salt	salt
100 g/4 oz pecorino cheese★, grated	1 cup grated pecorino cheese★
freshly ground black pepper	freshly ground black pepper

Cook the spaghetti in plenty of boiling salted water until *al dente*. Drain thoroughly, reserving 2 to 3 tablespoons of the cooking water. Place in a warmed serving dish, add the reserved liquid, pecorino and plenty of pepper. Toss well to mix and serve immediately.

SERVES 4

SPAGHETTI ALL'AMATRICIANA

Spaghetti with Tomato and Bacon Ragù

Metric/Imperial	American
1 tablespoon olive oil	1 tablespoon olive oil
100 g/4 oz lean bacon, diced	½ cup diced lean bacon
350 g/12 oz tomatoes, skinned and chopped	1½ cups skinned and chopped tomatoes
1 canned pimento	1 canned pimiento
400 g/14 oz spaghetti	14 oz spaghetti
salt	salt
50 g/2 oz pecorino or Parmesan cheese★, grated	½ cup grated pecorino or Parmesan cheese★

Heat the oil in a heavy pan, add the bacon and fry gently for 5 minutes until golden. Add the tomatoes and pimento and continue cooking over moderate heat for 10 minutes, stirring occasionally.

Meanwhile, cook the spaghetti in plenty of boiling salted water until *al dente*, then drain thoroughly. Remove the pimento from the ragù. Pile the spaghetti in a warmed serving dish, pour over the ragù and sprinkle with the cheese. Fold gently to mix and serve immediately.

SERVES 4

ABOVE: **Maccheroni alla pesarese; Spaghetti alla ciociàra; Spaghetti alla carbonara**

SPAGHETTI ALLA CARBONARA

Spaghetti with Egg and Bacon

Metric/Imperial	American
25 g/1 oz butter	2 tablespoons butter
100 g/4 oz bacon, diced	½ cup diced bacon
1 garlic clove, peeled	1 garlic clove, peeled
400 g/14 oz spaghetti	14 oz spaghetti
salt and freshly ground black pepper	salt and freshly ground black pepper
3 eggs, beaten	3 eggs, beaten
40 g/1½ oz Parmesan cheese★, grated	6 tablespoons grated Parmesan cheese★
40 g/1½ oz pecorino cheese★, grated	6 tablespoons grated pecorino cheese★

Melt the butter in a heavy pan, add the bacon and garlic, fry gently until browned, then remove the garlic from the pan.

Cook the spaghetti in plenty of boiling salted water until *al dente*. Drain thoroughly and add to the bacon. Stir well, then remove from the heat. Add the eggs, a pinch of pepper, half the Parmesan and half the pecorino. Toss until the eggs turn creamy yellow, then add the remaining cheeses. Toss again and serve immediately.

SERVES 4

SPAGHETTI ALLA CIOCIÀRA

Spaghetti with Olives

Metric/Imperial	American
150 ml/¼ pint olive oil	⅔ cup olive oil
1 yellow or green pepper, cored, seeded and sliced	1 yellow or green pepper, cored, seeded and sliced
3 tomatoes, skinned and chopped	3 tomatoes, skinned and chopped
salt and freshly ground black pepper	salt and freshly ground black pepper
100 g/4 oz black olives, halved and stoned	¾ cup pitted ripe olives
400 g/14 oz spaghetti	14 oz spaghetti
65 g/2½ oz pecorino or Parmesan cheese★, grated	⅝ cup grated pecorino or Parmesan cheese★

Heat the oil in a heavy pan, add the pepper, tomatoes and salt and pepper to taste. Cover and simmer gently for 20 minutes, stirring occasionally. Add the olives and cook for 5 minutes.

Meanwhile, cook the spaghetti in plenty of boiling salted water until *al dente*. Drain thoroughly and add to the sauce. Fold gently to mix, then pile into a warmed serving dish and sprinkle with the cheese. Serve immediately.

SERVES 4

The Romans are particularly fond of spaghetti. These recipes from Lazio illustrate how easy it is to serve spaghetti in more interesting ways than the ubiquitous *Spaghetti Bolognese*.

RIGHT: **Spaghetti alle vongole; Spaghetti alla napoletana; Pasta e ceci alla napoletana**

PASTA E CECI ALLA NAPOLETANA

Noodles with Chick Peas (Garbanzos)

Metric/Imperial	American
200 g/7 oz chick peas	1 cup garbanzos
1 litre/1¾ pints water	4¼ cups water
7 tablespoons olive oil	7 tablespoons olive oil
4 tomatoes, skinned and chopped	4 tomatoes, skinned and chopped
2 garlic cloves, peeled and crushed	2 garlic cloves, peeled and crushed
200 g/7 oz wholemeal or green fettuccine	7 oz wholemeal or green fettuccine
1 tablespoon chopped parsley	1 tablespoon chopped parsley
6 basil leaves, chopped	6 basil leaves, chopped
salt and freshly ground black pepper	salt and freshly ground black pepper

Soak the chick peas (garbanzos) in lukewarm water overnight. Drain and place in a large pan with the water, 3 tablespoons oil, the tomatoes and half the garlic. Bring to the boil, lower the heat, cover and simmer for 1 hour.

Add the fettuccine and cook for a further 15 minutes. Add the parsley, basil, remaining garlic and oil, and salt and pepper to taste. Serve immediately.

SERVES 4

SPAGHETTI ALLA PUTTANESCA

Spaghetti with Anchovies and Olives

Metric/Imperial	American
7 tablespoons olive oil	7 tablespoons olive oil
1 garlic clove, peeled and sliced	1 garlic clove, peeled and sliced
1 red pepper, cored, seeded and sliced	1 red pepper, cored, seeded and sliced
100 g/4 oz canned anchovies, drained and pounded	¼ lb canned anchovies, drained and pounded
400 g/14 oz tomatoes, skinned and chopped	1¾ cups skinned and chopped tomatoes
100 g/4 oz black olives, halved and stoned	¾ cup pitted ripe olives
1 tablespoon capers	1 tablespoon capers
400 g/14 oz spaghetti	14 oz spaghetti
salt	salt

Heat the oil in a heavy pan, add the garlic and red pepper and fry gently for 6 to 7 minutes until the garlic is well browned. Add the anchovies and cook, stirring until thoroughly blended.

Add the tomatoes, olives and capers and stir well. Cook gently for about 20 minutes, stirring occasionally.

Meanwhile, cook the spaghetti in plenty of boiling salted water until *al dente*. Drain thoroughly and pile into a warmed serving dish. Pour the sauce over the top and serve immediately.

SERVES 4

SPAGHETTI ALLA NAPOLETANA

Spaghetti with Tomato and Basil Sauce

Metric/Imperial	American
7 tablespoons olive oil	7 tablespoons olive oil
1 onion, peeled and chopped	1 onion, peeled and chopped
750 g/1¾ lb ripe tomatoes, chopped	3½ cups chopped tomatoes
1 tablespoon chopped basil	1 tablespoon chopped basil
salt and freshly ground black pepper	salt and freshly ground black pepper
400 g/14 oz spaghetti	14 oz spaghetti

Heat the oil in a heavy pan, add the onion and fry gently for 5 minutes. Add the tomatoes, basil and salt and pepper to taste. Cook gently for 30 minutes.

Meanwhile, cook the spaghetti in plenty of boiling salted water until *al dente*. Drain thoroughly and pile into a warmed serving dish. Pour the sauce over the top and serve immediately.

SERVES 4

SPAGHETTI ALLE VONGOLE

Spaghetti with Clams

Fresh mussels may be used instead of clams in the sauce for this recipe.

Metric/Imperial	American
1 kg/2 lb fresh clams, scrubbed	2 lb fresh clams, scrubbed
7 tablespoons water	7 tablespoons water
7 tablespoons olive oil	7 tablespoons olive oil
1 garlic clove, peeled and sliced	1 garlic clove, peeled and sliced
400 g/14 oz tomatoes, skinned and mashed	1¾ cups skinned and mashed tomatoes
400 g/14 oz spaghetti	14 oz spaghetti
salt and freshly ground black pepper	salt and freshly ground black pepper
1 tablespoon chopped parsley	1 tablespoon chopped parsley

Put the clams in a large pan with the water. Cook until the shells open, then remove the clams from their shells. Strain the cooking liquid and reserve.

Heat the oil in a heavy pan, add the garlic and fry gently for 5 minutes. Remove the garlic, then add the tomatoes and the reserved cooking liquid to the pan. Stir and simmer for 20 minutes.

Meanwhile, cook the spaghetti in plenty of boiling salted water until *al dente*. Drain thoroughly. Add the clams and parsley to the tomato sauce and heat through for 1 minute. Pile the spaghetti in a warmed serving dish, add the sauce and a pinch of pepper and fold gently to mix. Serve immediately.

SERVES 4

The majority of commercially made pasta comes from the city of Naples in Campania. According to the experts, the water in the city is exactly the right kind to make perfect pasta. The combination of hard wheat and water makes it unnecessary to include the eggs in commercial pasta (eggs are needed when making pasta at home as a binding agent), but many manufacturers include eggs because of popular demand.

ABOVE: **Pasta col broccolo; Rigatoni al forno; Pasta 'ncaciata**

RIGATONI AL FORNO
Baked Rigatoni

Metric/Imperial	American
1 thick slice stale bread	1 thick slice stale bread
150 g/5 oz minced beef	⅔ cup ground beef
75 g/3 oz pecorino cheese★, grated	¾ cup grated pecorino cheese★
1 egg, beaten	1 egg, beaten
1 tablespoon chopped parsley	1 tablespoon chopped parsley
1 garlic clove, peeled and crushed	1 garlic clove, peeled and crushed
salt and freshly ground black pepper	salt and freshly ground black pepper
4 tablespoons olive oil	¼ cup olive oil
150 g/5 oz sopressata sausage★, diced	⅔ cup diced sopressata sausage★
200 ml/⅓ pint red wine	1 cup red wine
400 g/14 oz tomatoes, skinned and chopped	1¾ cups skinned and chopped tomatoes
300 g/11 oz rigatoni	11 oz rigatoni
3 hard-boiled eggs, sliced	3 hard-cooked eggs, sliced
100 g/4 oz provola cheese★, sliced	¼ lb provola cheese★, sliced

Soak the bread in lukewarm water, then squeeze dry. Combine with the beef, one third of the pecorino, the egg, parsley, garlic and salt and pepper to taste. Stir well to mix, then shape into small balls, about the size of walnuts.

Heat the oil in a pan, add the sausage and meatballs and cook over moderate heat for 10 minutes. Add the wine and simmer until it has evaporated, then add the tomatoes and salt and pepper to taste. Lower the heat and simmer for 40 minutes.

Meanwhile, cook the rigatoni in plenty of boiling salted water until *al dente*. Drain thoroughly.

Line the bottom of a buttered deep ovenproof dish with a layer of sauce, cover with a layer of rigatoni, then sprinkle with pecorino. Cover with a layer of sliced egg, then a layer of provola. Continue with these layers until all the ingredients are used, finishing with a layer of sauce and a sprinkling of pecorino. Bake in a preheated moderately hot oven (200°C/400°F/Gas Mark 6) for 15 minutes. Serve hot.
SERVES 4

Cook the broccoli in boiling salted water for 15 minutes. Drain thoroughly.

Heat half the oil in a heavy pan, add the onion and fry gently for 5 minutes. Add the tomatoes and salt and pepper to taste, cover the pan and simmer for 30 minutes.

Heat the remaining oil in a separate pan, add the garlic and fry gently until browned. Add the anchovies and cook, stirring, until broken down. Add to the sauce with the raisins, broccoli and pine kernels. Cook for a further 5 minutes, stirring frequently. Meanwhile, cook the macaroni in boiling salted water until *al dente*. Drain thoroughly and pile into a warmed serving dish. Pour over the sauce, then add the basil and pecorino and fold gently to mix. Serve immediately.
SERVES 4

SICILY

PASTA 'NCACIATA

Tagliatelle with Ragù

Metric/Imperial	American
7 tablespoons olive oil	7 tablespoons olive oil
1 onion, peeled and chopped	1 onion, peeled and chopped
1 carrot, peeled and chopped	1 carrot, peeled and chopped
1 celery stick, chopped	1 celery stalk, chopped
1 garlic clove, peeled and thinly sliced	1 garlic clove, peeled and thinly sliced
800 g/1¾ lb tomatoes, skinned and mashed	3½ cups skinned and mashed tomatoes
225 g/8 oz minced veal	1 cup ground veal
100 g/4 oz chicken livers, minced	½ cup ground chicken livers
salt and freshly ground black pepper	salt and freshly ground black pepper
450 g/1 lb tagliatelle, broken into pieces	4 cups broken tagliatelle
2 hard-boiled eggs, sliced	2 hard-cooked eggs, sliced
100 g/4 oz mozzarella cheese★, cut into strips	¼ lb mozzarella cheese★, cut into strips
25 g/1 oz pecorino cheese★, grated	¼ cup grated pecorino cheese★

Heat the oil in a heavy pan, add the onion, carrot, celery and garlic and fry gently for 6 to 7 minutes. Add the tomatoes, veal, chicken livers and salt and pepper to taste. Cover the pan and simmer for 30 minutes.

Cook the tagliatelle in plenty of boiling salted water until *al dente*. Drain thoroughly, then spread a layer of tagliatelle in the bottom of a buttered ovenproof dish. Sprinkle with the ragù, then cover with a layer of egg slices and strips of mozzarella. Continue with these layers until all the ingredients are used, then sprinkle the pecorino on top. Bake in a preheated moderate oven (180°C/350°F/Gas Mark 4) for 20 minutes until golden brown. Serve immediately.
SERVES 6

The islands of Italy follow the southern style of cooking. Pasta is common fare, but both the Sicilians and the Sardinians have their own pasta dishes which are unique to each island.

SICILY

PASTA COL BROCCOLO

Macaroni with Broccoli

Metric/Imperial	American
350 g/12 oz broccoli	¾ lb broccoli
salt	salt
4 tablespoons olive oil	¼ cup olive oil
1 onion, peeled and sliced	1 onion, peeled and sliced
450 g/1 lb tomatoes, skinned and mashed	2 cups skinned and mashed tomatoes
freshly ground black pepper	freshly ground black pepper
1 garlic clove, peeled and crushed	1 garlic clove, peeled and crushed
6 canned anchovies, drained and soaked in milk	6 canned anchovies, drained and soaked in milk
40 g/1½ oz seedless raisins, soaked in lukewarm water for 15 minutes	4½ tablespoons seedless raisins soaked in lukewarm water for 15 minutes
40 g/1½ oz pine kernels	4½ tablespoons pine kernels
350 g/12 oz macaroni	¾ lb macaroni
4 basil leaves, chopped	4 basil leaves, chopped
75 g/3 oz pecorino cheese★, grated	¾ cup grated pecorino cheese★

VERMICELLI ALLA SIRACUSANA
Vermicelli Syracuse Style

Metric/Imperial	American
1 green pepper	1 green pepper
7 tablespoons olive oil	7 tablespoons olive oil
2 garlic cloves, peeled	2 garlic cloves, peeled
1 aubergine, diced	1 eggplant, diced
400 g/14 oz tomatoes, skinned and mashed	1¾ cups skinned and mashed tomatoes
1 tablespoon capers	1 tablespoon capers
8 black olives, halved and stoned	8 ripe olives, halved and pitted
1 tablespoon chopped basil	1 tablespoon chopped basil
4 canned anchovies, drained and soaked in milk	4 canned anchovies, drained and soaked in milk
freshly ground black pepper	freshly ground black pepper
400 g/14 oz vermicelli	14 oz vermicelli
75 g/3 oz pecorino cheese★, grated	¾ cup grated pecorino cheese★

Grill (broil) the pepper under a preheated medium grill (broiler), turning frequently, until charred. Peel off the skin. Cut the pepper in half, remove the core and seeds and slice the flesh.

Heat the oil in a heavy pan, add the garlic and fry gently until browned. Discard the garlic. Add the aubergine (eggplant) and tomatoes and simmer for 10 minutes. Add the pepper, capers, olives, basil, anchovies and pepper to taste. Simmer for a further 10 minutes, stirring frequently.

Meanwhile cook the vermicelli in plenty of boiling salted water until *al dente*. Drain thoroughly and pile into a warmed serving dish. Pour over the sauce, sprinkle with pecorino and fold gently to mix. Serve immediately.

SERVES 4

MACCHERONI AL POMODORO
Macaroni in Tomato Sauce

This recipe gives instructions for making macaroni from fresh pasta; commerical dried pasta can alternatively be used.

Metric/Imperial	American
PASTA:	PASTA:
400 g/14 oz plain flour	3½ cups all-purpose flour
salt	salt
4 eggs, beaten	4 eggs, beaten
1 tablespoon olive oil	1 tablespoon olive oil
TOMATO SAUCE:	TOMATO SAUCE:
7 tablespoons olive oil	7 tablespoons olive oil
2 garlic cloves, peeled and crushed	2 garlic cloves, peeled and crushed
800 g/1¾ lb tomatoes, skinned and mashed	3½ cups skinned and mashed tomatoes
freshly ground black pepper	freshly ground black pepper
1 tablespoon chopped parsley	1 tablespoon chopped parsley

To make the pasta: sift the flour and a pinch of salt onto a work surface, then make a well in the centre. Add the eggs and oil and mix together to a smooth dough.

Flatten the dough with a rolling pin and roll into a paper-thin sheet. Fold the dough over on itself several times, then cut it into fairly long slices. Cut these slices into strips about 6 to 7 cm/2½ inches long. Wind the strips tightly around a large knitting needle (pin) to make small cylindrical shapes. Place the macaroni in a single layer on a cloth sprinkled with flour, then leave to dry for 1 hour.

Meanwhile, make the sauce: heat the oil in a heavy pan, add the garlic and fry gently for 5 minutes. Add the tomatoes and salt and pepper to taste. Bring to the boil, lower the heat and simmer for 30 minutes.

Meanwhile cook the macaroni in plenty of boiling salted water until *al dente*. Drain thoroughly and pile into a warmed serving dish. Pour over the sauce, sprinkle with the parsley and serve immediately.

SERVES 4

ABOVE: **Vermicelli alla siracusana; Culingiones; Maccheroni al pomodoro**

CULINGIONES
Ravioli with Ragù

Metric/Imperial

PASTA:

450 g/1 lb pasta all'uovo
  (see page 16:
  1½ × quantity)

FILLING:

300 g/11 oz pecorino
  cheese★, grated

400 g/14 oz fresh spinach,
  cooked, well drained and
  chopped

2 eggs, beaten

pinch of saffron powder

salt and freshly ground
  black pepper

RAGÙ:

3 tablespoons olive oil

1 onion, peeled and chopped

100 g/4 oz fatty bacon or
  belly pork, chopped

225 g/8 oz minced veal

1 tablespoon chopped
  parsley

6 basil leaves, chopped

575 g/1¼ lb tomatoes,
  skinned and mashed

75 g/3 oz pecorino cheese★,
  grated, to serve

American

PASTA:

1 lb pasta all'uovo (see
  page 16: 1½ × quantity)

FILLING:

2¾ cups grated pecorino
  cheese★

2 cups chopped cooked
  spinach, well drained

2 eggs, beaten

pinch of saffron powder

salt and freshly ground
  black pepper

RAGÙ:

3 tablespoons olive oil

1 onion, peeled and chopped

½ cup chopped fatty bacon or
  pork slices

1 cup ground veal

1 tablespoon chopped
  parsley

6 basil leaves, chopped

2½ cups skinned and mashed
  tomatoes

¾ cup grated pecorino
  cheese★, to serve

Make the pasta and leave to stand for about 1 hour.

Meanwhile make the filling: put the cheese, spinach, half the beaten egg, and the saffron in a bowl. Season with salt and pepper to taste and mix thoroughly.

Flatten the dough with a rolling pin and roll out to a paper-thin sheet. Put heaped teaspoonfuls of the filling over one half of the dough at regular intervals, about 5 cm/2 inches apart.

Brush the other half of the dough with the remaining egg and place loosely over the filling. Press the pasta between the filling firmly to seal. Cut between the filling to make small squares of ravioli, using a tooth-edged rotary cutter. Place the squares in a single layer on a cloth sprinkled with flour, and leave to dry for about 1 hour.

Meanwhile make the ragù: heat the oil in a heavy pan, add the onion and bacon and fry gently for 5 minutes. Add the veal, parsley and basil and cook for 10 minutes. Add the tomatoes and salt and pepper to taste. Simmer for 1 hour, adding a little warm water if the sauce is too thick.

Cook the ravioli in plenty of boiling salted water for 5 minutes or until they rise to the surface. Remove from the pan with a slotted spoon and pile into a warmed serving dish. Pour over the ragù and sprinkle with the pecorino. Serve immediately.

SERVES 4

Rice, Polenta, Gnocchi

The rice fields of the Po Valley are reminiscent of the paddy fields of the East, for the Italians use the river for irrigation in exactly the same way as the Chinese, making Vercelli in Piemonte the greatest rice-producing area in Italy. Piedmontese rice has long been regarded as the best quality. Not surprisingly, Italians in the north are bigger rice eaters than those in central and southern Italy who eat more pasta.

Rice is not eaten as a vegetable accompaniment in Italy, but as a first course (*primo piatto*). The one exception to this is the famous saffron-coloured *Risotto alla milanese* (see page 32), which is the traditional accompaniment to *Ossibuchi alla milanese* (see page 52).

A risotto should have a creamy consistency, the rice should be moist (*all'onda*), and the grains of rice should be separate and *al dente*. This perfect end result is achieved by cooking gently and adding the liquid to the rice gradually during cooking, waiting for it to be absorbed by the rice before adding more. Frequent stirring is also essential to avoid sticking. Unlike rice dishes in other countries, a risotto is always made with short-grain rice which is very absorbent. Long-grain, Patna or short-grain pudding rice are not suitable. The best types of rice to use are *arborio*, *superfino* or *avorio*; all of these can be purchased at Italian specialist shops. *Avorio* is ideal for the novice risotto maker as it is pre-fluffed. *Carnaroli* is said to be the best of all the rices, but it is unusual to find it outside Italy.

There is more to risotto than rice, however, as quite apart from a well-flavoured homemade stock, a risotto can have other ingredients added such as vegetables, chicken livers, meat and Parmesan cheese, making it almost a meal in itself. Even leftover risotto is made into a dish in its own right, usually in the form of a fried 'cake', which is served turned out of the frying pan (skillet) and cut into portions. Risotto can also be used to make croquettes (*suppli*) and rissoles (*arancini*).

Rice for plain boiling (*fino*) is available in most good supermarkets and delicatessens outside Italy labelled 'Italian rice'.

Polenta is another staple foodstuff of northern Italy; it is rarely eaten in the regions south of Rome. A basic *polenta* is made with *polenta* or maize flour and salted water. Maize flour is known as *granturco* in Italy, and it is available here in specialist and health food shops. The varieties available are very coarse, medium coarse and fine; the coarser the flour is, the more yellow in colour. Whatever the type of flour used, *polenta* is invariably made in a special large copper pan called a *paiolo*. The method is always the same – the flour is added gradually to a pan of hot water and the mixture is stirred constantly throughout the cooking time with a long wooden stick to prevent lumps forming.

Plain boiled *polenta* can be rather bland, so it is often served with a strong-flavoured sauce or with grated cheese. Some of the best *polenta* dishes are those that have been cooked twice; the *polenta* is left to cool, then fried or grilled (broiled) and served with a sauce. Cold *polenta*, cut into slices or chunks, is eaten as bread in some parts of northern Italy.

Gnocchi are also eaten as a first course (*primo piatto*). They are little 'dumplings' most often made of potatoes or flour, or a mixture of the two; sometimes this can be combined with meat, cheese or spinach (*gnocchi verde*). The shapes of gnocchi also vary, from perfect spheres to elongated cylinders. Some of them are stamped into rounds with small cutters, then baked in layers in the oven.

A type of gnocchi called *Canderli* (see page 33) which comes from the region of Trentino-Alto Adige is made with bread. Gnocchi are usually served with a sauce of some kind – tomato sauce or a simple mixture of butter and grated Parmesan cheese are common. Very small gnocchi are sometimes added to *brodo*, and are even used in goulash-type casseroles and stews, particularly in north-eastern regions.

LIGURIA

FARINATA

Chick Pea (Garbanzos) Bake

Metric/Imperial	American
1.5 litres/2½ pints water	6¼ cups water
450 g/1 lb chick pea flour	4 cups garbanzos flour
salt	salt
6–8 tablespoons olive oil	6–8 tablespoons olive oil
freshly ground black pepper	freshly ground black pepper

Pour the water into a large heavy pan, then gradually stir in the flour. Add salt to taste. Cook over gentle heat for 1 hour, stirring frequently and skimming the surface with a slotted spoon occasionally; the mixture should be smooth and quite thick.

Pour the mixture into an oiled roasting pan and level the surface. Sprinkle the oil over the surface. Bake in a preheated moderately hot oven (200°C/400°F/Gas Mark 6) for 30 minutes until golden brown.

Sprinkle liberally with pepper and serve immediately.

SERVES 6

POLENTA CÔNCIA
Polenta with Fontina

Metric/Imperial	American
2 litres/3½ pints water	9 cups water
300 g/11 oz polenta (yellow maize flour)	1⅔ cups polenta (yellow maize flour)
salt and freshly ground black pepper	salt and freshly ground black pepper
225 g/8 oz fontina cheese★, diced	1½ cups diced fontina cheese★
50 g/2 oz Parmesan cheese★, grated	½ cup grated Parmesan cheese★
150 g/5 oz butter, melted	⅔ cup butter, melted

Bring the water to the boil in a large pan, add the flour gradually, then add salt and pepper to taste and stir well to mix. Add the fontina and cook very gently for 45 minutes, stirring frequently.

Pour the polenta into a shallow dish and sprinkle with the Parmesan and a little pepper. Pour the melted butter over the top and serve immediately.

SERVES 4 TO 6

RISO ALLA NOVARESE
Rice Novara Style

Metric/Imperial	American
50 g/2 oz butter	¼ cup butter
275 g/10 oz brown or white rice	1⅓ cups brown or white rice
750 ml/1¼ pints water	3 cups water
salt	salt
4 canned anchovies, drained and roughly chopped	4 canned anchovies, drained and roughly chopped
1 garlic clove, peeled and chopped	1 garlic clove, peeled and chopped
1 tablespoon chopped parsley	1 tablespoon chopped parsley
juice of 1 lemon	juice of 1 lemon
7 tablespoons olive oil	7 tablespoons olive oil
1 truffle or a few button mushrooms, thinly sliced	1 truffle or a few button mushrooms, thinly sliced

Melt the butter in a flameproof casserole, add the rice and stir over moderate heat for 2 to 3 minutes. Add the water and a little salt and bring to the boil.

Cover the casserole and transfer to a preheated moderate oven (180°C/350°F/Gas Mark 4). Bake for 20 minutes, without stirring, until the rice has absorbed the liquid.

Meanwhile, pound the anchovies, garlic and parsley to a paste, using a mortar and pestle. Add the lemon juice and oil gradually, stirring until evenly blended.

To serve: fold the anchovy mixture gently into the rice. Spread the truffle or mushrooms over the top. Serve immediately.

SERVES 4

LEFT: **Farinata; Riso alla novarese**

RISOTTO ALLA MILANESE

This is the traditional accompaniment to Ossibuchi alla milanese (see page 52)

Metric/Imperial	American
150 g/5 oz butter	⅔ cup butter
½ onion, chopped	½ onion, chopped
salt and freshly ground black pepper	salt and freshly ground black pepper
7 tablespoons dry white wine	7 tablespoons dry white wine
1 litre/1¾ pints hot beef stock	4¼ cups hot beef stock
400 g/14 oz rice	2 cups rice
¼ teaspoon saffron powder	¼ teaspoon saffron powder
100 g/4 oz Parmesan cheese★, grated	1 cup grated Parmesan cheese★
4 tablespoons cream	¼ cup cream

Melt half the butter in a large heavy pan, add the onion and a little pepper and fry gently until golden. Add the wine and 7 tablespoons of the stock. Boil until reduced by half.

Add the rice and cook for 5 minutes, stirring constantly, then add the saffron and salt and pepper to taste. Continue cooking for 20 minutes, stirring in the hot stock a cup at a time as the liquid is absorbed, until the rice is tender.

Remove from the heat, stir in the remaining butter, the Parmesan and cream and leave to stand for 1 minute. Serve hot.

SERVES 4 TO 6

RISOTTO ALLA VALTELLINESE

Risotto with Cabbage and Beans

Metric/Imperial	American
200 g/7 oz broad beans, fresh or frozen	1 cup lima beans, fresh or frozen
1 medium cabbage, shredded	1 medium cabbage, shredded
300 g/11 oz rice	1½ cups rice
salt	salt
75 g/3 oz butter	⅓ cup butter
few sage leaves, chopped	few sage leaves, chopped
50 g/2 oz Parmesan cheese★, grated	½ cup grated Parmesan cheese★
freshly ground black pepper	freshly ground black pepper

Parboil the broad (lima) beans, if fresh, for 2 to 3 minutes, then drain. Put the cabbage, rice and a little salt in a large heavy pan with plenty of water and simmer for 10 minutes. Add the beans and cook for a further 10 minutes.

Drain the rice and vegetables and spoon into a warmed serving dish. Melt the butter in a small pan with the sage, then pour over the rice. Add the Parmesan and a little pepper and fold gently to mix. Serve immediately.

SERVES 4 TO 6

RISOTTO ARROSTO

Baked Risotto

Metric/Imperial	American
100 g/4 oz butter	½ cup butter
½ onion, chopped	½ onion, chopped
225 g/8 oz salsiccia a metro★, chopped	1 cup chopped salsiccia a metro★
150 g/5 oz shelled peas	scant 1 cup shelled peas
2 artichoke hearts, chopped	2 artichoke hearts, chopped
25 g/1 oz mushrooms, chopped	¼ cup chopped mushrooms
400 ml/⅔ pint beef stock	2 cups beef stock
salt and freshly ground black pepper	salt and freshly ground black pepper
400 g/14 oz rice	2 cups rice
1 litre/1¾ pints water	4¼ cups water
75 g/3 oz Parmesan cheese★, grated	¾ cup grated Parmesan cheese★

Melt 3 tablespoons butter in a large flameproof casserole, add the onion and fry gently until golden. Stir in the sausage and fry, stirring, for 3 minutes. Add the peas, artichoke hearts, mushrooms, stock and salt and pepper to taste. Cook gently for 20 minutes.

Meanwhile, put the rice and water in a separate pan, add salt to taste and boil for 5 minutes. Drain, then add to the vegetable mixture with the Parmesan and remaining butter.

Bake in a preheated moderately hot oven (200°C/400°F/Gas Mark 6) for 20 minutes until a golden-brown crust forms on the top of the rice. Serve immediately.

SERVES 4 TO 6

Strangolapreti, literally translated, means 'strangled priests'. These little spinach-flavoured dumplings seem to have created confusion over the exact meaning of their name. Some Italians tell the story of priests being strangled to death by these dumplings because of the heaviness of the mixture, whereas others say the priests were so delighted by their taste that they literally choked to death with the sheer pleasure of tasting them!

STRANGOLAPRETI
Spinach Dumplings

Metric/Imperial	American
225 g/8 oz dry crumbly bread, diced	½ lb dry crumbly bread, diced
150 ml/¼ pint boiling water	⅔ cup boiling water
225 g/8 oz fresh spinach, cooked, well drained and chopped	1 cup chopped cooked spinach, well drained
3 eggs, beaten	3 eggs, beaten
150 g/5 oz plain flour	1¼ cups all–purpose flour
pinch of grated nutmeg	pinch of grated nutmeg
salt and freshly ground black pepper	salt and freshly ground black pepper
TO SERVE:	TO SERVE:
50 g/2 oz butter	¼ cup butter
few sage leaves, chopped	few sage leaves, chopped
75 g/3 oz Parmesan cheese★, grated	¾ cup grated Parmesan cheese★

Put the bread in a shallow bowl and pour over the boiling water. Cover with a saucer or plate, put a weight on top and leave to stand overnight.

Drain the bread, then squeeze it as dry as possible. Mix the bread with the spinach, eggs, flour, nutmeg and salt and pepper to taste.

Drop the mixture a spoonful at a time into a large pan of boiling salted water and boil for 5 minutes or until the dumplings rise to the surface.

Meanwhile, melt the butter with the sage in a separate pan. Remove the dumplings from the pan with a slotted spoon and place in a warmed serving dish.

Serve immediately, with the melted butter and Parmesan cheese.

SERVES 4 TO 6

CANDERLI
Dumplings with Salami and Bacon

Metric/Imperial	American
350 g/12 oz dry crumbly bread, diced	¾ lb dry crumbly bread, diced
150 ml/¼ pint milk	⅔ cup milk
2 tablespoons olive oil	2 tablespoons olive oil
100 g/4 oz smoked bacon, chopped	½ cup chopped smoked bacon
50 g/2 oz salami, chopped	¼ cup chopped salami
50 g/2 oz plain flour	½ cup all–purpose flour
1 tablespoon chopped parsley	1 tablespoon chopped parsley
1 egg, beaten	1 egg, beaten
1 egg yolk	1 egg yolk
salt	salt
1.5 litres/2½ pints beef stock	6¼ cups beef stock
Tomato sauce (see page 28) to serve	Tomato sauce (see page 28) to serve

Put the bread in a bowl, pour over the milk and leave to soften for about 1½ hours.

Heat the oil in a small pan, add the bacon and salami and fry gently for 5 minutes. Remove from the pan with a slotted spoon and transfer to a bowl. Squeeze the bread as dry as possible, then add to the bowl with the flour, parsley, egg, egg yolk and salt to taste. Mix until thoroughly combined, then shape the mixture into dumplings, the size of walnuts.

Bring the stock to the boil in a large pan. Add the dumplings a few at a time and simmer until they rise to the surface. Remove from the pan with a slotted spoon and place in a warmed serving dish. Serve hot, with tomato sauce.

SERVES 4 TO 6

ABOVE: **Canderli; Risotto alla valtellinese; Strangolapreti**

Canderli **are believed to be German in origin, as are many dishes from the northern regions of Italy. They are a type of gnocchi made with bread rather than the usual potatoes or flour.** *Canderli* **are purely local to Trentino–Alto Adige, and it is unlikely they will be found in other Italian regions.**

GNOCCHI DELLA CARNIA

Potato Dumplings with Parmesan

Metric/Imperial	American
900 g/2 lb potatoes	2 lb potatoes
salt	salt
225 g/8 oz plain flour	2 cups all-purpose flour
100 g/4 oz Parmesan cheese★, grated	1 cup grated Parmesan cheese★
2 eggs, beaten	2 eggs, beaten
75 g/3 oz sugar	6 tablespoons sugar
pinch of grated nutmeg	pinch of grated nutmeg
50 g/2 oz butter, melted	¼ cup butter, melted
pinch of ground cinnamon	pinch of ground cinnamon

Cook the potatoes in boiling salted water until tender, then peel and mash. Blend in the flour, half the cheese, the eggs, 2 tablespoons sugar, the nutmeg and a pinch of salt. Shape the mixture into large round dumplings.

Drop the dumplings a few at a time into a large pan of boiling salted water and boil for 15 minutes. Remove from the pan with a slotted spoon and pile into a warmed serving dish. Sprinkle over the butter, remaining cheese and sugar, and the cinnamon. Serve immediately.

SERVES 6

RISOTTO ALLA SBIRAGLIA

Chicken Risotto

Metric/Imperial	American
1 × 1 kg/2-2½ lb oven-ready chicken	1 × 2-2½ lb oven-ready chicken
2 litres/3½ pints water	9 cups water
2 celery sticks	2 celery stalks
2 onions, peeled	2 onions, peeled
2 carrots, peeled	2 carrots, peeled
salt and freshly ground black pepper	salt and freshly ground black pepper
3-4 tablespoons olive oil	3-4 tablespoons olive oil
7 tablespoons white wine	7 tablespoons white wine
350 g/12 oz tomatoes, skinned and mashed	1½ cups skinned and mashed tomatoes
450 g/1 lb rice	2¼ cups rice
75 g/3 oz butter, softened	⅓ cup softened butter
75 g/3 oz Parmesan cheese★, grated	¾ cup grated Parmesan cheese★

Remove the bones from the chicken and place them in a large pan with the water. Add 1 celery stick (stalk), 1 onion and 1 carrot and season liberally with salt and pepper. Bring to the boil, lower the heat, cover and simmer for 1½ hours. Strain the stock and keep hot.

Meanwhile, dice the chicken meat, removing all skin. Finely chop the remaining vegetables. Heat the oil in a large heavy pan, add the vegetables and fry gently until lightly coloured. Add the chicken and fry for a further 5 minutes, stirring constantly, then add the wine and boil until it evaporates.

Add the tomatoes and salt and pepper to taste. Cover and cook gently for 20 minutes, adding a little of the chicken stock if the mixture becomes dry.

Stir in the rice, then add 200 ml/⅓ pint/1 cup chicken stock. Cook for 20 to 25 minutes until the rice is just tender, adding a little more stock to moisten, as necessary.

Remove from the heat, add the butter and Parmesan and fold gently to mix. Serve immediately.

SERVES 6

RISOTTO DI SCAMPI

Risotto with Scampi

If fresh scampi is unobtainable, frozen, thawed, scampi may be used instead. Omit the first stage of precooking the scampi in seasoned water and use a fish stock or light chicken stock as the cooking liquor for the risotto.

Metric/Imperial	American
450 g/1 lb fresh scampi	1 lb fresh scampi
1 litre/1¾ pints water	4¼ cups water
1 bay leaf, chopped	1 bay leaf, chopped
2 garlic cloves, peeled and chopped	2 garlic cloves, peeled and chopped
salt	salt
3 tablespoons olive oil	3 tablespoons olive oil
75 g/3 oz butter, softened	⅓ cup softened butter
1 onion, peeled and chopped	1 onion, peeled and chopped
400 g/14 oz rice	2 cups rice
3-4 tablespoons white wine	3-4 tablespoons white wine
freshly ground black pepper	freshly ground black pepper

Wash the scampi and put them in a pan with the water, bay leaf, garlic and a pinch of salt. Bring to the boil and cook for 5 minutes. Remove the scampi from the water with a slotted spoon and peel off the shells. Return the shells to the water and boil for a further 5 minutes, then strain and keep the stock hot.

Meanwhile, dice the scampi. Heat the oil and 2 tablespoons butter in a large heavy pan, add the onion and fry gently until golden. Stir in the rice, then add the wine. Cook gently for 15 minutes, stirring frequently. Add the stock a little at a time to moisten as necessary during cooking.

Add the scampi, remaining butter and salt and pepper to taste, then cook for a further 5 to 10 minutes until the rice is just tender. Remove from the heat, leave to stand for 1 minute, then serve.

SERVES 4 TO 6

BELOW: **Risotto alla sbiraglia; Risotto di scampi**

RISOTTO ALLA FIORENTINA

Risotto with Meat

Metric/Imperial	American
2 tablespoons olive oil	2 tablespoons olive oil
65 g/2½ oz butter, softened	5 tablespoons softened butter
1 onion, peeled and sliced	1 onion, peeled and sliced
225 g/8 oz minced beef	1 cup ground beef
100 g/4 oz kidneys, sliced	½ cup sliced kidneys
1 chicken liver, sliced	1 chicken liver, sliced
400 g/14 oz tomatoes, skinned and mashed	1¾ cups skinned and mashed tomatoes
salt and freshly ground black pepper	salt and freshly ground black pepper
400 g/14 oz rice	2 cups rice
1 litre/1¾ pints hot beef stock	4¼ cups hot beef stock
75 g/3 oz Parmesan cheese★, grated	¾ cup grated Parmesan cheese★

Heat the oil and half the butter in a large heavy pan, add the onion and fry gently for 5 minutes until golden. Add the beef, kidneys and chicken liver, increase the heat and fry until browned, stirring constantly. Add the tomatoes and salt and pepper to taste, lower the heat and cook gently for 30 minutes.

Stir in the rice, then add half the stock. Cook for 20 minutes, stirring frequently and adding the remaining stock to moisten as necessary. Remove from the heat, stir in the remaining butter and the Parmesan and fold gently to mix. Leave to stand for 2 minutes, then serve.
SERVES 4 TO 6

RISOTTO ALLA PARMIGIANA

Risotto with Parmesan

Metric/Imperial	American
100 g/4 oz butter, softened	½ cup softened butter
½ onion, peeled and chopped	½ onion, peeled and chopped
freshly ground black pepper	freshly ground black pepper
3–4 tablespoons white wine	3–4 tablespoons white wine
400 g/14 oz rice	2 cups rice
1 litre/1¾ pints hot beef stock	4¼ cups hot beef stock
100 g/4 oz Parmesan cheese★, grated	1 cup grated Parmesan cheese★

Melt half the butter in a heavy pan, add the onion and fry gently until soft. Add pepper to taste, then the wine and boil until it evaporates.

Add the rice and cook, stirring, for 2 to 3 minutes so that it absorbs the mixture. Cook gently for 20 to 25 minutes until the rice is just tender, stirring frequently and adding the hot stock a little at a time to moisten.

Remove from the heat, add the remaining butter and the Parmesan and fold gently to serve.
SERVES 4 TO 6

The northern Italians eat rice dishes and risottos to the same extent as the Italians in the south eat pasta. Every Italian cook has a favourite method of cooking risotto, sometimes serving it as a simple rice dish with grated Parmesan cheese as its only accompaniment, other times turning it into a substantial meal in itself by adding chicken, meat, offal (variety meats), fish or vegetables.

Pizzas, Pies & Savoury Doughs

It is believed that pizzas were originally invented by the Neapolitans to use up leftover bread dough. The classic recipe for this delicious food is the *Pizza Napoletana* (see page 38). In Italy, pizzas are made fresh to order in *pizzerie*, special bakeries equipped with brick ovens that reach exceptionally high temperatures so that the dough is 'set' almost immediately on entering the oven.

Pizzas can very easily be baked at home in conventional ovens, and many Italian housewives regularly make their own. There is no special secret to success, since the base is usually an ordinary bread dough made with yeast, and the choice of toppings is endless and can be varied according to the ingredients which happen to be to hand. Plain (all purpose) flour is used for the dough and either dried or fresh (compressed) yeast, whichever is more convenient. Be sure to knead the dough very thoroughly until springy, smooth and elastic (10 to 15 minutes should be long enough) before rolling and stretching it out to the required shape and thickness. Pizzas do not necessarily have to be round; some are large ovals, some are square or rectangular, and others known as *pizzette* are baked as individual circles about the diameter of the top rim of a teacup – these are often served as an *antipasto*.

The thickness of the dough is quite important, since dough that has been rolled too thin will be hard and brittle, but if the dough is too thick, the pizza will be yeasty and indigestible. Roll the dough out to a thickness between 5 mm–1 cm/$\frac{1}{4}$–$\frac{1}{2}$ inch, and try to keep the edges slightly thicker than the middle to prevent the topping from running off the dough during baking. Some cooks place a plain flan ring around the dough on the baking (cookie) sheet to help contain the pizza as it rises and cooks.

The filling should then be spread to within 1 cm/$\frac{1}{2}$ inch of the edge and the remaining ingredients placed on top. Always preheat the oven before putting the pizza in, and serve straight from the oven.

There are many variations of the classic pizza throughout southern Italy and in parts of the north. *Pizza Campofranco* (see page 38) is made with a yeast pastry rather than a bread dough and has a double crust, with a filling in the middle. Pies of this kind are quite common, so too are individual pasties like the traditional *Calzone alla pugliese* made with pizza dough. Savoury doughs are quite often fried in Italy. The dough is usually stamped into rounds and deep-fried to make individual pizzas.

ABOVE: **Sardenaira**

UMBRIA

TORTA SUL TESTO
Fried Pizza Dough

This recipe is used as a basis for the other pizzas. The quantities given below yield 450 g/1 lb dough. If a recipe requires less, reduce the quantities accordingly.

Metric/Imperial	American
15 g/$\frac{1}{2}$ oz dried yeast	2 packages (4 teaspoons) active dry yeast
120 ml/4 fl oz warm water	$\frac{1}{2}$ cup warm water
450 g/1 lb plain flour	4 cups all-purpose flour
salt	salt
3 tablespoons olive oil	3 tablespoons olive oil

Dissolve the yeast in the water. Sift the flour and a little salt onto a working surface. Stir in the yeast liquid, then add the oil and enough lukewarm water to make a smooth dough. Cover with oiled plastic wrap and leave to rise in a warm place for 30 minutes.

Flatten the dough with a rolling pin, then divide in half. Roll each piece out into a circle, about 1 cm/$\frac{1}{2}$inch thick. Heat a large iron griddle or frying pan (skillet). When it is very hot, add one of the dough circles and cook, without additional fat, turning and pricking the dough with a fork, until crisp and golden. Repeat with the remaining dough. Serve in place of bread.

SERVES 4

LOMBARDY

FITASCETTA
Onion Pizza

Metric/Imperial	American
75 g/3 oz butter	$\frac{1}{3}$ cup butter
750 g/1$\frac{1}{2}$ lb onions, peeled and finely sliced	6 cups finely sliced onions
salt	salt
450 g/1 lb pizza dough (see left)	1 lb pizza dough (see left)
1 tablespoon caster sugar	1 tablespoon sugar

Melt the butter in a large frying pan (skillet), add the onions and fry gently for 30 minutes, stirring frequently. Remove from the heat, then add salt to taste.

Knead the dough until smooth and elastic, then flatten with a rolling pin and roll out to a 25 cm/10 inch circle, 1 cm/$\frac{1}{2}$ inch thick. Place the circle on an oiled baking (cookie) sheet. Spread the onions over the dough, then sprinkle with the sugar. Leave to rise in a warm place for 20 minutes. Bake in a preheated moderately hot oven (200°C/400°F/Gas Mark 6) for 30 to 35 minutes. Serve hot.

SERVES 6 TO 8

SARDENAIRA

Tomato and Anchovy Pizza

Metric/Imperial	American
7 tablespoons olive oil	7 tablespoons olive oil
450 g/1 lb onions, peeled and sliced	4 cups sliced onions
salt and freshly ground black pepper	salt and freshly ground black pepper
450 g/1 lb tomatoes, chopped	2 cups chopped tomatoes
450 g/1 lb pizza dough (see opposite)	1 lb pizza dough (see opposite)
100 g/4 oz canned anchovy fillets, drained and cut in half lengthways	4 oz canned anchovy fillets, drained and cut in half lengthways
100 g/4 oz black olives, halved and stoned	1 cup ripe olives, halved and pitted
few garlic cloves, peeled and slivered	few garlic cloves, peeled and slivered
1 tablespoon chopped basil	1 tablespoon chopped basil

Heat 3 tablespoons oil in a heavy pan, add the onions and fry gently for 10 minutes. Add salt and pepper to taste, then remove from the heat.

Place the tomatoes in a saucepan. Add salt and pepper to taste and simmer for 10 to 15 minutes until reduced to a pulp; strain.

Knead the dough until smooth and elastic, then flatten with a rolling pin and roll out to a 25 cm/10 inch circle, 1 cm/½ inch thick. Place the circle in a shallow baking tin to fit. Leave to rise in a warm place for 20 minutes.

Spread the onions and tomato pulp over the dough. Arrange the anchovy fillets and olive halves on top. Add slivers of garlic according to taste, then sprinkle with the basil and remaining oil. Bake in a preheated moderately hot oven (200°C/400°F/Gas Mark 6) for 35 to 40 minutes. Serve hot.

SERVES 6 TO 8

Pizza bakers in Naples are often cooks, artists and actors all in one. They can be seen through the windows of *pizzerie* pulling, stretching and kneading the pizza dough, then spreading and sprinkling the topping over with a flourish. The pizza tray is then pushed into the oven on a special long-handled shovel and the pizza baker starts his show all over again.

RIGHT: **Pizza Campofranco; Pizza Napoletana; Focaccia salata**

PIZZA CAMPOFRANCO
Ham and Cheese Pizza Pie

Metric/Imperial	American
DOUGH:	DOUGH:
25 g/1 oz fresh yeast	1 cake compressed yeast
4–5 tablespoons lukewarm milk	4–5 tablespoons lukewarm milk
300 g/11 oz plain flour	2¾ cups all-purpose flour
½ teaspoon salt	½ teaspoon salt
25 g/1 oz sugar	2 tablespoons sugar
150 g/5 oz butter, diced	⅔ cup butter, diced
2 eggs, beaten	2 eggs, beaten
FILLING:	FILLING:
2 tablespoons olive oil	2 tablespoons olive oil
2 ripe tomatoes, skinned, seeded and chopped	2 ripe tomatoes, skinned, seeded and chopped
freshly ground black pepper	freshly ground black pepper
6 basil leaves, finely chopped	6 basil leaves, finely chopped
175 g/6 oz mozzarella cheese★, sliced	6 oz mozzarella cheese★, sliced
150 g/5 oz raw smoked or cooked ham, cut into thin strips	⅔ cup shredded raw smoked or cooked ham
50 g/2 oz pecorino cheese★, grated	½ cup grated pecorino cheese★
TO FINISH:	TO FINISH:
beaten egg to glaze	beaten egg to glaze
basil leaves to garnish	basil leaves to garnish

To make the dough: dissolve the yeast in the milk. Sift the flour and salt onto a work surface. Stir in the sugar and make a well in the centre. Add the butter, eggs and the dissolved yeast and work the ingredients together to give a smooth dough. Knead well until pliable, then shape into a ball.

Put the dough in a bowl sprinkled with flour, cover with a clean cloth and leave to rise at room temperature for 2 hours or until doubled in bulk.

Meanwhile, make the filling: heat the oil in a pan, add the tomatoes and cook over moderate heat for 5 minutes. Add salt and pepper to taste, then remove from the heat.

Knead the dough for 5 minutes, then break off two-thirds and flatten with a rolling pin. Roll out to a thin circle and use to line an oiled 23 cm/9 inch loose-bottomed cake tin (springform pan). Spread the tomatoes on top of the dough, then sprinkle with the basil. Cover with half the mozzarella and the ham, then top with the remaining mozzarella and the pecorino cheese.

Flatten the remaining dough and roll out to a circle to fit the top of the pizza. Place the circle over the filling, then press the edges firmly together to seal. Leave in a warm place to rise for 30 to 40 minutes. Brush the top with beaten egg. Bake in a preheated moderately hot oven (200°C/400°F/Gas Mark 6) for 15 minutes, then lower the temperature to (190°C/375°F/Gas Mark 5) and bake for a further 20 minutes. Serve immediately, garnished with basil.
SERVES 8

PIZZA NAPOLETANA
Pizza with Mozzarella, Tomatoes and Anchovies

Metric/Imperial	American
4 tablespoons olive oil	4 tablespoons olive oil
350 g/12 oz tomatoes, chopped	1½ cups chopped tomatoes
salt and freshly ground black pepper	salt and freshly ground black pepper
450 g/1 lb pizza dough (see page 36)	1 lb pizza dough (see page 36)
175 g/6 oz mozzarella cheese★, sliced	6 oz mozzarella cheese★, sliced
8 canned anchovy fillets, drained and cut in half lengthways	8 canned anchovy fillets, drained and cut in half lengthways
2 teaspoons chopped basil or oregano	2 teaspoons chopped basil or oregano

Heat half the oil in a pan, add the tomatoes and cook over moderate heat for 5 minutes. Season with salt and pepper to taste and remove from the heat.

Knead the dough until smooth and elastic, then flatten with a rolling pin and roll out to a 25 cm/10 inch circle.

Place the circle on an oiled baking (cookie) sheet. Spread the tomato pulp over the dough, leaving a 1 cm/½ inch margin around the edge. Place the cheese slices on the tomatoes. Arrange the anchovy fillets in a lattice pattern on top. Sprinkle with the basil or oregano, the remaining oil and salt and pepper to taste. Leave to rise in a warm place for 20 minutes.

Bake in a preheated moderately hot oven (200°C, 400°F/Gas Mark 6) for 25 minutes. Serve hot.
SERVES 4

FOCACCIA SALATA
Tomato and Herb Pizza

Metric/Imperial	American
225 g/½ lb pizza dough (see page 36)	½ lb pizza dough (see page 36)
3 tomatoes, skinned and chopped	3 tomatoes, skinned and chopped
2 garlic cloves, peeled and slivered	2 garlic cloves, peeled and slivered
1 tablespoon chopped marjoram	1 tablespoon chopped marjoram
2 tablespoons olive oil	2 tablespoons olive oil
salt and freshly ground black pepper	salt and freshly ground black pepper

Knead the dough until smooth and elastic, then flatten with a rolling pin and roll out to a 25 cm/10 inch circle. Place the circle on an oiled baking (cookie) sheet. Make little grooves with the fingertips at regular intervals in the dough, then fill the grooves with the tomatoes and garlic. Sprinkle with the marjoram, oil and salt and pepper to taste. Leave in a warm place to rise for 20 minutes. Bake in a preheated moderately hot oven (200°C/400°F/Gas Mark 6) for 25 minutes. Serve hot or cold.
SERVES 4

Pizza Napoletana is the pizza best known outside Italy, mainly because it was the emigré Neapolitans who first opened *pizzerie* in England and the United States and introduced the world to their colourful cheese and tomato topped dough. Tomatoes are an essential ingredient for *Pizza Napoletana*, but sometimes when fresh tomatoes are not available in winter, the Neapolitans make *salsa pizzaiola*, a sauce topping made with canned tomatoes. Mozzarella cheese has exactly the right melting qualities for pizza toppings, and is another vital ingredient for *pizza Napoletana*; if it is difficult to obtain, Bel Paese or gruyère can be used instead.

Egg & Cheese Dishes

Eggs are important in the Italian kitchen, both as an ingredient in cooking, and as cooked dishes in their own right. Eggs are used to give more substance to soups as in *Zuppa alla pavese* (see page 12) and to give more body to sauces. They are also used for binding mixtures like stuffings for ravioli and cannelloni. *Frittelle* (crêpes) made with eggs are popular, so too are *frittate* (omelets). These are more like Spanish omelets, with all kinds of different ingredients incorporated into the basic mixture. Eggs are also used in Italian cakes and desserts; perhaps the most famous of these is *Zabaione* (see page 92), which is made from egg yolks.

Cheese is used in countless Italian dishes, as so many of the Italian cheeses have good melting properties. The different types of cheeses are described in the glossary (see page 93). The most common Italian cooking cheeses which are available in this country are *mozzarella*, Parmesan and *ricotta*. *Mozzarella* is a southern cheese most frequently used for its unique melting properties

on pizzas. It is also deep-fried, as in *Mozzarella in carrozza* (see page 43), which literally translated means '*mozzarella* in a carriage', and is a kind of deep-fried cheese sandwich. *Provatura fritta* (see page 43) is a famous Roman dish of deep-fried cheese; these days it is usually made with *mozzarella*, *provatura* cheese is almost impossible to obtain, even in Italy. *Crostini* is another Roman cheese speciality – *mozzarella* baked on bread, then garnished with anchovies.

Ricotta, the Italian soft curd cheese, is often used in cheese croquettes and in stuffings for *frittelle* (crêpes). It is probably used as much in sweet dishes as it is in savoury ones, mainly because its rather bland flavour lends itself to such strong spices as nutmeg, cloves and cinnamon, and to liqueurs and candied fruits. It is often used in this way as a filling for pies and pastries. Parmesan is a perfect cooking cheese as its flavour marries well with many different ingredients. It should ideally always be bought in the piece and freshly grated at the time of using.

FRITTATA ALL 'ARETINA

Omelet in Tomato and Herb Sauce

Metric/Imperial	American
6 eggs	6 eggs
1 tablespoon plain flour	1 tablespoon all-purpose flour
65 g/2½ oz dried breadcrumbs	⅔ cup dried bread crumbs
salt and freshly ground black pepper	salt and freshly ground black pepper
4 tablespoons olive oil	¼ cup olive oil
1 onion, peeled and chopped	1 onion, peeled and chopped
1 celery stick, chopped	1 celery stalk, chopped
1 bunch parsley, chopped	1 bunch parsley, chopped
3 basil leaves, chopped	3 basil leaves, chopped
350 g/12 oz tomatoes, skinned and chopped	1½ cups skinned and chopped tomatoes

Put the eggs in a bowl with the flour, breadcrumbs and salt and pepper to taste. Beat well to mix.

Heat the oil in a frying pan (skillet). Pour in the mixture and tilt the pan so that the mixture covers the base. Fry the omelet on both sides until set, shaking the pan frequently to prevent the mixture from sticking. Remove from the pan and leave to cool slightly, then cut into slices.

Add the onion, celery and herbs to the pan with a little more oil if necessary; fry gently for 5 minutes. Add the tomatoes and cook gently for 10 minutes, then return the slices of omelet to the pan and heat through for 5 minutes. Serve immediately.
SERVES 4

FRITTATA CON ERBA TARGONE

Tarragon Omelet

Metric/Imperial	American
1 small bunch tarragon	1 small bunch tarragon
6 eggs	6 eggs
2 tablespoons cream	2 tablespoons cream
salt and freshly ground black pepper	salt and freshly ground black pepper
50 g/2 oz butter	¼ cup butter
tarragon leaves to garnish	tarragon leaves to garnish

Discard the stems from the tarragon and chop the leaves. Put the eggs in a bowl with the cream, tarragon and salt and pepper to taste. Beat well to mix.

Melt the butter in a frying pan (skillet). Pour in the mixture and tilt the pan so that the mixture covers the base. Fry the omelet on both sides until set, shaking the pan frequently to prevent the mixture from sticking. Serve immediately, garnished with tarragon.
SERVES 4

FRITTATA DI CARCIOFI

Artichoke Omelet

Metric/Imperial	American
3 globe artichokes	3 globe artichokes
plain flour for coating	all-purpose flour for coating
4 tablespoons olive oil	4 tablespoons olive oil
salt and freshly ground black pepper	salt and freshly ground black pepper
50 g/2 oz butter	¼ cup butter
6 eggs, beaten	6 eggs, beaten

Wash the artichokes, discard the hard outer leaves, then cut off and discard two-thirds of the tops with a sharp knife. Cut the artichokes in half, remove the choke then cut into slivers and coat with flour. Heat the oil in a frying pan (skillet) and fry the artichokes until well browned. Drain on absorbent kitchen paper and sprinkle with salt and pepper.

Melt the butter in a frying pan (skillet), add the artichokes, then pour in the beaten eggs and sprinkle with more salt and pepper. Tilt the pan so that the mixture covers the base. Cook on both sides until set, shaking the pan frequently to prevent the omelet from sticking. Serve immediately.

SERVES 4

FRITTATA ALLA BOLOGNESE

Omelet with Parmesan

Metric/Imperial	American
6 eggs, separated	6 eggs, separated
25 g/1 oz plain flour	¼ cup all-purpose flour
3–4 tablespoons water	3–4 tablespoons water
150 g/5 oz Parmesan cheese★, grated	1¼ cups grated Parmesan cheese★
1 tablespoon chopped parsley	1 tablespoon chopped parsley
salt and freshly ground black pepper	salt and freshly ground black pepper
50 g/2 oz butter	¼ cup butter

Put the egg yolks in a bowl with the flour and beat well with a wooden spoon until smooth. Stir in the water, then add the Parmesan, parsley and salt and pepper to taste; beat well.

Beat the egg whites until stiff and carefully fold into the omelet mixture. Melt the butter in a large frying pan (skillet), pour in the mixture and tilt the pan so that the mixture covers the base.

Fry on both sides until the omelet is set, shaking the pan frequently to prevent sticking. Serve immediately.

SERVES 4

The Italian *frittata* is best described as an omelet, yet it is nothing like the light fluffy French *omelette* which is folded over during cooking. The Italians make *frittate* rather like a cross between a pancake (crêpe) and an omelet: they cook them until set on both sides in the frying pan (skillet) like a pancake mixture. They are rarely served plain, but are full of ingredients, especially vegetables and herbs, cheese and sometimes meat or leftovers. They are always served flat on the plate and eaten cut into slices or wedges. *Frittate* are often eaten cold, in which case they are an excellent idea for picnics in summer.

Truffles are a highly-prized fungus which grow underground in the root systems of certain trees. They are gathered with the help of specially trained dogs who have a keen sense of smell. The dogs sniff out the truffles, which are then carefully removed from the ground by the truffle hunter with a special tool.

FRITTATA DI TARTUFI

Omelet with Truffles or Mushrooms

Black truffles are used in Italy, but if these are unavailable or prohibitively expensive, mushrooms make an acceptable alternative.

Metric/Imperial	American
6 eggs	6 eggs
4 tablespoons cream	$\frac{1}{4}$ cup cream
salt and freshly ground black pepper	salt and freshly ground black pepper
100 g/4 oz black truffles or mushrooms, chopped	$\frac{1}{4}$ lb black truffles or mushrooms, chopped
40 g/1$\frac{1}{2}$ oz butter	3 tablespoons butter
juice of $\frac{1}{2}$ lemon	juice of $\frac{1}{2}$ lemon
parsley sprig to garnish	parsley sprig to garnish

Put the eggs in a bowl with the cream and salt and pepper to taste. Beat well, then stir in the truffles or mushrooms.

Melt the butter in a frying pan (skillet). Pour in the mixture and tilt the pan so that the mixture covers the base. Fry on both sides until set, shaking the pan frequently to prevent the omelet from sticking. Remove from the heat and sprinkle with the lemon juice. Serve immediately, garnished with parsley.

SERVES 4

FRITTATA AL BASILICO

Omelet with Basil and Cheese

Metric/Imperial	American
6 eggs	6 eggs
50 g/2 oz pecorino cheese★, grated	$\frac{1}{2}$ cup grated pecorino cheese★
50 g/2 oz coarsely chopped basil	1$\frac{1}{2}$ cups coarsely chopped basil
salt and freshly ground black pepper	salt and freshly ground black pepper
50 g/2 oz butter	$\frac{1}{4}$ cup butter

Put all the ingredients, except the butter, in a bowl and beat well.

Melt the butter in a frying pan (skillet). Pour in the mixture and tilt the pan so that the mixture covers the base. Fry on both sides until set, shaking the pan frequently to prevent the omelet from sticking. Serve immediately.

SERVES 4

PROVATURA FRITTA
Fried Cheese Cubes

Metric/Imperial
*400 g/14 oz provatura or
  mozzarella cheese★, cut
  into 3.5 cm/1½ inch cubes
plain flour for coating
1–2 eggs, beaten
dried breadcrumbs for
  coating
vegetable oil for deep-frying
sage or basil leaves to
  garnish*

American
*14 oz provatura or
  mozzarella cheese★, cut
  into 1½ inch cubes
all-purpose flour for coating
1–2 eggs, beaten
dried bread crumbs for
  coating
vegetable oil for deep-frying
sage or basil leaves to
  garnish*

Coat the cheese lightly in flour, dip into the beaten eggs, then coat with breadcrumbs. Dip again into the beaten eggs and coat with a second layer of breadcrumbs.

Deep-fry the cubes, a few at a time, in the hot oil until golden brown. Drain on absorbent kitchen paper while frying the remainder. Serve hot, garnished with sage or basil.

BELOW: **Frittata di tartufi;
Frittata al basilico;
Provatura fritta**

SERVES 4

MOZZARELLA IN CAROZZA
Deep-Fried Cheese Sandwiches

Metric/Imperial
*4 thick slices mozzarella
  cheese★
8 slices of bread, crusts
  removed
1–2 tablespoons plain flour
2 eggs, beaten
pinch of salt
vegetable oil for shallow
  frying*

American
*4 thick slices mozzarella
  cheese★
8 slices of bread, crusts
  removed
1–2 tablespoons all-purpose
  flour
2 eggs, beaten
pinch of salt
vegetable oil for shallow
  frying*

Trim the mozzarella slices to fit the bread. Sandwich each slice of cheese between 2 slices of bread, pressing firmly. Sprinkle the inside edges with a little flour and cold water and press together firmly to seal.

Put the eggs and salt in a large shallow dish. Add the sandwiches and turn to coat evenly. Leave to stand for 20 minutes.

Pour the oil into a frying pan (skillet) to a depth of 1 cm/½ inch. Place over moderate heat. Fry the sandwiches in the hot oil until golden brown on both sides, then drain on absorbent kitchen paper. Serve hot.

SERVES 4

Fish & Shellfish

With an extensive coastline, well-stocked lakes, rivers and streams, it is hardly surprising that Italy regards fish as one of her staple foodstuffs. In general the Italians treat their fish simply, avoiding the rich and heavy types of sauces with wine and cream, of which the French are so fond. The Italians prefer to concentrate more on the fish itself.

Simple methods like grilling (broiling), barbecuing, baking and marinating are the most popular ways of cooking fish. Small fry such as fresh anchovies and sardines are usually served simply deep-fried with a garnish of lemon. Even the fish stews and soups are the simple kind, with little more than a basic tomato sauce flavoured with onions, garlic and herbs, in which to cook the fish.

The variety of seafood obtainable in Italy is infinite and many types are unique to that part of the Mediterranean. Amongst the most popular dishes are *baccalà* (salt fish), eels and various hearty fish soups.

Baccalà in Italy is white fish – usually cod – that has been salted and dried. It is sometimes also called *stoccafisso* by Italians and this can be misleading as stockfish is an unsalted dried fish. Before using *baccalà* it must be soaked in several changes of cold water to remove excess saltiness. The length of soaking time will vary according to whether the *baccalà* has been soaked before buying and if so, how long. The Venetian *Baccalà mantecato* is probably the most famous of all dishes made with *baccalà*. It is like the French *brandade de morue*, a kind of creamed paste or spread, made by pounding the *baccalà* to break it down, then mixing it with olive oil, garlic and seasonings to taste. It is served with pieces of fried bread or *polenta*, which diners use to scoop up the fish.

Eels are also common throughout Italy and can be cooked in many different ways. The Italians particularly like to spit roast, bake or stew them, or serve them casseroled, sometimes in a simple tomato sauce or with wine. Marinated eels are a popular Christmas dish.

In the south, where the local population relies more heavily on fish than in the more fertile northern regions, each fishing village has its own version of the substantial fish soup which is similar to the French *bouillabaisse*. There is the famous *burrida* from Genoa, the *brodetto* of Abbruzzi, Marche and Campania, the *cassola* from Sicily, or the *zuppa di pesce* from Apulia. Each region is justifiably proud of its own version, with its particular varieties of fish and flavouring ingredients.

ABOVE: **Datteri di mare in sughetto; Gamberetto all'erba; Friscieü di gianchetti**

LIGURIA

FRISCIEÜ DI GIANCHETTI

Whitebait Fritters

Metric/Imperial	American
200 g/7 oz plain flour	1¾ cups all-purpose flour
salt and freshly ground black pepper	salt and freshly ground black pepper
300 ml/½ pint lukewarm water (approximately)	1¼ cups lukewarm water (approximately)
450 g/1 lb whitebait	1 lb whitebait
vegetable oil for deep-frying	vegetable oil for deep-frying
4 lemon wedges, to serve	4 lemon wedges, to serve

Sift the flour with a pinch of salt and pepper into a bowl. Add enough lukewarm water to obtain a thick coating batter, beating vigorously until smooth. Add the whitebait to the batter and stir until thoroughly coated.

Heat the oil in a deep-fryer. Add the whitebait, a few at a time, and deep-fry until golden brown and crisp. Drain on absorbent kitchen paper and keep hot while frying the remainder. Serve hot with lemon wedges.
SERVES 4

FRIULI-VENEZIA GIULIA

GAMBERETTO ALL'ERBA

Shrimps with Herbs

Metric/Imperial	American
4 tablespoons olive oil	¼ cup olive oil
4 garlic cloves, peeled	4 garlic cloves, peeled
575 g/1¼ lb cooked shelled shrimps	1¼ lb cooked shelled shrimp
5 basil leaves, finely chopped	5 basil leaves, finely chopped
5 marjoram leaves, finely chopped	5 marjoram leaves, finely chopped
3–4 parsley sprigs, finely chopped	3–4 parsley sprigs, finely chopped
pinch of paprika pepper	pinch of paprika pepper
pinch of salt	pinch of salt
3–4 tablespoons dry white wine	3–4 tablespoons dry white wine
marjoram sprigs to garnish	marjoram sprigs to garnish

Heat the oil in a flameproof casserole, add the garlic and fry gently until browned. Remove the garlic, then add the shrimps, herbs, paprika, salt and wine and cook gently until the shrimps are heated through.

Serve immediately, garnished with marjoram.
SERVES 4 TO 6

Mix the oil, lemon juice and onion together and season liberally with salt and pepper. Place the fish in a shallow dish, pour over the marinade and leave to marinate for 1 hour, turning from time to time.

Drain the fish thoroughly and dry on absorbent kitchen paper. Coat with flour. Dip in the beaten eggs, then coat with breadcrumbs, pressing them firmly into the fish.

Melt the butter in a frying pan (skillet), add the fish and fry gently until golden brown on both sides and cooked through. Transfer to a warmed serving platter and pour over the cooking juices. Serve immediately.

SERVES 4

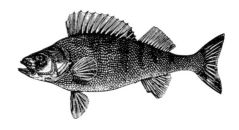

FRIULI-VENEZIA GIULIA

DATTERI DI MARE IN SUGHETTO

Mussels on Croûtons

Metric/Imperial	American
1.5 kg/3 lb mussels	3 lb mussels
150 ml/¼ pint olive oil (approximately)	⅔ cup olive oil (approximately)
½ onion, peeled and chopped	½ onion, peeled and chopped
7 tablespoons dry white wine	7 tablespoons dry white wine
salt and freshly ground black pepper	salt and freshly ground black pepper
4 slices bread	4 slices bread
parsley sprigs to garnish	parsley sprigs to garnish

Scrub the mussels under cold running water, then place in a large bowl. Cover with cold water and leave to stand for 30 minutes. Drain and discard any with open shells.

Heat 7 tablespoons oil in a large pan, add the onion and fry gently for 5 minutes, stirring constantly. Add the mussels and wine to the pan and season with salt and pepper to taste. Cover and cook for about 5 minutes until the shells open. Discard any that have not opened.

Meanwhile, fry the bread in the remaining oil until crisp and golden on both sides. Cut each slice into 4 pieces and arrange in individual soup plates. Spoon the mussels over the bread and pour over the cooking juices. Serve immediately, garnished with parsley.

SERVES 4

LOMBARDY

PESCE PERSICO ALLA COMASCA

Marinated Perch

Metric/Imperial	American
4 tablespoons olive oil	¼ cup olive oil
juice of 1 lemon	juice of 1 lemon
1 small onion, peeled and chopped	1 small onion, peeled and chopped
salt and freshly ground black pepper	salt and freshly ground black pepper
4 perch, skinned and filleted	4 perch, skinned and fileted
plain flour for coating	all-purpose flour for coating
2 eggs, beaten with a pinch of salt	2 eggs, beaten with a pinch of salt
dried breadcrumbs for coating	dried bread crumbs for coating
75 g/3 oz butter	⅓ cup butter

CIECHE ALLA PISANA
Eel au Gratin

Metric/Imperial	American
7 tablespoons olive oil	7 tablespoons olive oil
4 garlic cloves, peeled and crushed	4 garlic cloves, peeled and crushed
4 sage leaves, chopped	4 sage leaves, chopped
1 kg/2 lb eels, cleaned	2 lb eels, cleaned
200 ml/$\frac{1}{3}$ pint warm water	1 cup warm water
salt and freshly ground black pepper	salt and freshly ground black pepper
4 eggs	4 eggs
50 g/2 oz dried breadcrumbs	$\frac{1}{2}$ cup dried bread crumbs
75 g/3 oz Parmesan cheese★, grated	$\frac{3}{4}$ cup grated Parmesan cheese★
juice of $\frac{1}{2}$ lemon	juice of $\frac{1}{2}$ lemon
sage leaves to garnish	sage leaves to garnish

Heat the oil in a flameproof casserole, add the garlic and sage and fry gently until browned. Add the eels, cover and cook for 5 minutes. Add the warm water and salt and pepper to taste. Cover and cook in a preheated moderate oven (180°C/350°F/Gas Mark 4) for 30 minutes or until the eels are tender.

Put the eggs in a bowl with the breadcrumbs, Parmesan, lemon juice and a pinch of salt and pepper. Stir well to mix. Spread this mixture over the eels, then grill (broil) under a preheated hot grill (broiler) until a crisp crust has formed. Serve immediately, garnished with sage.

SERVES 4

TRIGLIE ALLA LIVORNESE
Red Mullet Casserole

Metric/Imperial	American
olive oil for shallow-frying	olive oil for shallow-frying
2 garlic cloves, peeled and sliced	2 garlic cloves, peeled and sliced
1 small onion, peeled and chopped	1 small onion, peeled and chopped
450 g/1 lb tomatoes, skinned and chopped	2 cups skinned and chopped tomatoes
salt and freshly ground black pepper	salt and freshly ground black pepper
2 red mullet, each weighing about 450 g/1 lb, cleaned	2 red mullet, each weighing about 1 lb, cleaned
plain flour for coating	all-purpose flour for coating
1 tablespoon chopped parsley	1 tablespoon chopped parsley

Heat 3 tablespoons oil in a flameproof casserole, add the garlic and fry gently for 5 minutes. Discard the garlic, add the onion and fry gently for 5 minutes. Add the tomatoes and season liberally with salt and pepper. Cover and simmer for 15 minutes.

Meanwhile, heat 4 tablespoons oil in a frying pan (skillet). Coat the fish with flour and fry in the hot oil until golden brown on all sides. Remove and drain on absorbent kitchen paper, then sprinkle with salt and pepper.

Add the mullet to the casserole and simmer for 5 minutes. Sprinkle with parsley and serve immediately.

SERVES 4

LEFT: **Cieche alla pisana;
Triglie in graticola**

Capitoni eels from
Grosseto in Tuscany are
the most highly prized of
all the eels, mainly
because their plump flesh
is so sweet and succulent.
They are exported all
over Italy, but
particularly to Rome,
where they are sold in the
fish markets on
Christmas Eve for the
traditional Christmas
Eve meal. The eels used
in the recipe for *Cieche
alla pisana* (opposite) are
a different kind from
capitoni. Cieche (the
blind) are blind elvers
which are caught at the
mouth of the river Arno,
near the town of Pisa.
They are peculiar to this
area and considered a
great delicacy, although
the recipe can equally
well be made with any
kind of eel.

MARCHE

BRODETTO ALL'
ANCONETANA

Fish Stew Ancona Style

*For this chowder, choose a selection of fish and shellfish to
provide a variety of textures and flavours. Red or grey
mullet, bass, sole, halibut, shrimp, clams and mussels are
popular ingredients in Italy.*

Metric/Imperial	American
1.5 kg/3 lb mixed fish and	*3 lb mixed fish and*
shellfish, cleaned	*shellfish, cleaned*
3–5 tablespoons olive oil	*3–5 tablespoons olive oil*
plain flour for coating	*all-purpose flour for coating*
1 onion, peeled and chopped	*1 onion, peeled and chopped*
3 garlic cloves, peeled	*3 garlic cloves, peeled*
2 bay leaves	*2 bay leaves*
1 piece of canned pimento	*1 piece of canned pimiento*
450 g/1 lb tomatoes, skinned	*2 cups skinned and chopped*
and chopped	*tomatoes*
1 tablespoon chopped	*1 tablespoon chopped*
parsley	*parsley*
salt and freshly ground	*salt and freshly ground*
black pepper	*black pepper*
2 tablespoons wine vinegar	*2 tablespoons wine vinegar*
6 slices toasted bread	*6 slices toasted bread*

If the shellfish is raw, place in a pan with 2 tablespoons
of the oil and cook until the shells open. Remove the
shells and set the shellfish aside. Cut the other fish into
serving pieces and coat with flour.

Heat the remaining oil in a large flameproof
casserole, add the onion, garlic, bay leaves and pimento. Cook gently for 10 minutes, then discard the
garlic. Add the tomatoes, parsley and salt and pepper to
taste. Simmer for 20 minutes, stirring occasionally,
then strain.

Return the sauce to the casserole and add all the fish,
except the shellfish. Cover and simmer for 15 minutes
until the fish is tender. Add the shellfish and vinegar
and cook for a further 5 minutes.

Place a slice of toast in each individual soup bowl and
spoon over the fish stew. Serve immediately.
SERVES 6

ABRUZZI & MOLISE

TRIGLIE IN
GRATICOLA

Marinated Mullet

Metric/Imperial	American
1 garlic clove, peeled and	*1 garlic clove, peeled and*
crushed	*crushed*
1 tablespoon chopped	*1 tablespoon chopped*
parsley	*parsley*
2 dried bay leaves, crumbled	*2 dried bay leaves, crumbled*
7 tablespoons olive oil	*7 tablespoons olive oil*
salt and freshly ground	*salt and freshly ground*
black pepper	*black pepper*
2 grey or red mullet, each	*2 grey or red mullet, each*
weighing about 450 g/	*weighing about 1 lb,*
1 lb, cleaned with head	*cleaned with head and*
and tail intact	*tail intact*
dried bay leaves to garnish	*dried bay leaves to garnish*

Mix the garlic, parsley, bay leaves and oil with a little
salt and pepper. Put the mullet in a shallow dish, pour
over the marinade and leave to marinate for 1 hour,
turning the fish over occasionally.

Score the fish, making a criss-cross pattern, and cook
under a preheated hot grill (broiler) for 10 minutes on
each side, brushing frequently with the marinade.
Serve immediately, garnished with bay leaves.
SERVES 4

Meat Dishes

In the past, meat was not considered to be one of the staple foodstuffs of Italy – fish, pasta, vegetables and cheese were more widely consumed. Today, however, the quantity of meat eaten, particularly veal and pork, is quite considerable.

Beef is eaten more in the north of the country than elsewhere, for the rich pasturelands and alpine slopes breed excellent cattle. By and large these cattle are bred more for their milk than their meat, but a certain amount of good quality beef does find its way to the table. Oxen are used as working animals in Italy, and some of the beef is therefore tougher than non-Italians are used to, but the flavoursome stews of the north, with their long slow cooking, are eminently suitable for this kind of beef. Italians prefer to eat good quality beef as steaks, either plain or charcoal grilled (broiled).

Veal is a very popular meat in Italy, and there are countless recipes using it. The different kinds of veal to choose from include *vitello da latte*; this is meat from calves slaughtered when only a few weeks old, which were therefore entirely milk-fed. This is the most expensive and highly prized veal, and it is particularly suitable for veal escalopes. Meat from older calves from six to nine months is known as *vitello*, and this is the most common type of veal on sale in Italy and other countries. *Vitellone* is neither veal nor beef, but what some butchers call 'baby beef' and it is not suitable for escalopes. Apart from the numerous ways in which they serve escalopes, Italians also like to serve other cuts of veal in casseroles, as in *Ossibuchi alla milanese* (see page 52), and in roasts, such as *Arrosto di vitello al latte* (see page 52).

Lamb and kid are popular roasting meats, especially in the central regions around Rome and *abbacchio* (whole spit-roasted lamb) and *capretto* (whole spit-roasted kid) are common sights in these areas. Roast joints of young (spring) lamb are also popular, so too is the occasional casserole or stew.

Pork is very popular and the Italians are as fond of eating the fresh meat as they are of eating it cured, in the form of hams, bacon, sausages and salami. Spit-roasting whole young pigs, known as *porchetta* or *porceddu* is another, much-favoured, way of eating pork.

Offal (variety meats) are used a great deal. The Italians waste very little that is edible, so recipes for sausages, rissoles, meat loaves, stuffings and *ragù* often combine offal (variety meats) with minced (ground) veal, beef or pork.

PIEMONTE & VALLE D'AOSTA

BRASATO DI BUE AL BAROLO

Beef Casseroled in Barolo Wine

Metric/Imperial	American
1 kg/2 lb piece topside or top rump	2 lb piece beef top round or top rump
1 bottle Barolo or other red wine	1 bottle Barolo or other red wine
2 onions, peeled and chopped	2 onions, peeled and chopped
2 carrots, peeled and chopped	2 carrots, peeled and chopped
1 celery stick, chopped	1 celery stalk, chopped
1 garlic clove, peeled and thinly sliced	1 garlic clove, peeled and thinly sliced
1 bay leaf	1 bay leaf
1 rosemary sprig	1 rosemary sprig
pinch of dried thyme	pinch of dried thyme
1 cinnamon stick	1 cinnamon stick
2 whole cloves	2 whole cloves
4 tablespoons olive oil	$\frac{1}{4}$ cup olive oil
2 tablespoons tomato purée	2 tablespoons tomato paste
3–4 tablespoons beef stock	3–4 tablespoons beef stock
salt and freshly ground black pepper	salt and freshly ground black pepper
1 small glass brandy	1 small glass brandy

Put the meat in a large bowl with the wine, vegetables, herbs and spices. Leave to marinate in a cool place for 12 hours.

Drain the meat thoroughly, reserving the marinade. Heat the oil in a flameproof casserole and fry the meat over brisk heat, turning, until browned on all sides. Add the reserved marinade, vegetables, herbs and spices and cook over moderate heat for 10 minutes.

Mix the tomato purée (paste) with the stock, then add to the pan with salt and pepper to taste. Lower the heat, cover and simmer gently for 2 to 2$\frac{1}{2}$ hours until the meat is tender.

Drain the meat and keep hot. Work the cooking liquid in an electric blender or through a sieve (strainer). Return to the casserole, add the brandy and heat through. Slice the meat and arrange on a warmed serving platter. Pour over the sauce and serve immediately.

SERVES 4

RIGHT: **Brasato di bue al barolo**

CARBONATA VALDOSTANA

Beef Casserole, Valle d'Aosta Style

Metric/Imperial	American
750 g/1¾ lb stewing beef, cut into large chunks	1¾ lb stewing beef, cut into large chunks
plain flour for coating	all-purpose flour for coating
40 g/1½ oz beef dripping or 3 tablespoons oil	3 tablespoons beef dripping or oil
1 onion, peeled and chopped	1 onion, peeled and chopped
300 ml/½ pint robust red wine	1¼ cups robust red wine
salt and freshly ground black pepper	salt and freshly ground black pepper

Coat the meat with flour. Heat the dripping or oil in a flameproof casserole, add the meat and fry over brisk heat until browned on all sides. Remove the meat with a slotted spoon and set aside.

Add the onion to the casserole and fry gently for 5 minutes. Return the meat to the casserole, then add the wine and salt and pepper to taste. Cover and simmer for 2 hours or until the meat is tender. Stir a little water into the casserole if it becomes dry during cooking. Serve hot, with polenta (see page 31).

SERVES 4

COSTATA DI MANZO ALLA VALTELLINESE

Braised Beef Valtellina Style

Metric/Imperial	American
4 large, thin slices beef topside	4 large, thin slices beef top round
salt and freshly ground black pepper	salt and freshly ground black pepper
350 g/12 oz mushrooms, thinly sliced	3 cups thinly sliced mushrooms
8 tomatoes, skinned and chopped	8 tomatoes, skinned and chopped
100 g/4 oz butter	½ cup butter
6–8 tablespoons beef stock	6–8 tablespoons beef stock
450 g/1 lb small pickling onions, peeled	1 lb baby onions, peeled

Sprinkle the meat slices with salt and pepper to taste. Divide the mushrooms and tomatoes equally between the beef slices, placing it in the centre. Roll up each slice, enclosing the filling, and tie securely with string.

Melt the butter in a flameproof casserole, add the beef rolls and spoon over the butter and stock. Cover and simmer gently for 1 hour, basting occasionally.

Meanwhile, boil the onions in salted water for 10 minutes. Drain and add to the casserole. Cook for a further 30 minutes or until the meat and onions are tender.

Remove the string from the meat and transfer the meat and onions to a serving dish. Pour over the cooking juices and serve immediately.

SERVES 4

POLPETTE ALLA FIORENTINA
Beef Rissoles

Metric/Imperial	American
350 g/12 oz cooked minced beef	1½ cups ground cooked beef
2 garlic cloves, peeled and crushed	2 garlic cloves, peeled and crushed
2 potatoes, boiled and mashed	2 potatoes, boiled and mashed
1 tablespoon chopped parsley	1 tablespoon chopped parsley
75 g/3 oz Parmesan cheese★, grated	¾ cup grated Parmesan cheese★
1 stale bread roll, soaked in milk and squeezed dry	1 stale bread roll, soaked in milk and squeezed dry
salt and freshly ground black pepper	salt and freshly ground black pepper
1–2 eggs, beaten	1–2 eggs, beaten
dried breadcrumbs for coating	dried bread crumbs for coating
vegetable oil for shallow-frying	vegetable oil for shallow-frying
parsley sprigs to garnish	parsley sprigs to garnish

Put the beef in a bowl with the garlic, potato, parsley, Parmesan, bread and salt and pepper to taste. Add enough beaten egg to bind the mixture and stir until the ingredients are thoroughly combined. Shape the mixture into oval rissoles, then coat in breadcrumbs.

Heat the oil in a frying pan (skillet). Add the rissoles and fry over moderate heat until golden brown on all sides. Drain on absorbent kitchen paper. Serve hot, garnished with parsley.

SERVES 4

Tuscan beef ranks amongst the finest in the world, and *Bistecca alla fiorentina*, charcoal-grilled (broiled) steak, is one of the greatest of all Italian dishes. In Tuscany, only beef from the Chianina breed of cattle is used for this dish. It is a huge rib steak which is always served plain – any sauce or accompaniment would only detract from the superb flavour and tender texture of the meat. Chianina cattle are reputed to be the oldest breed of cattle in the world, and probably the tallest and heaviest. They are noted for their speedy growth – by the time other breeds of cattle would reach a comparable size to the Chianina, their meat would be tough and sinewy.

BELOW: **Bistecchine alla napoletana; Polpette alla fiorentina; Stufato di manzo alla fiorentina**

STUFATO DI MANZO ALLA FIORENTINA

Tuscan Beef Stew

Metric/Imperial	American
3–4 tablespoons olive oil	3–4 tablespoons olive oil
2 garlic cloves, peeled and crushed	2 garlic cloves, peeled and crushed
1 teaspoon chopped rosemary	1 teaspoon chopped rosemary
750 g/1¾ lb stewing beef, cut into cubes	1¾ lb stewing beef, cut into cubes
pinch of ground mixed spice	pinch of ground allspice
salt and freshly ground black pepper	pinch of ground cinnamon
7 tablespoons red wine	salt and freshly ground black pepper
5 tablespoons tomato purée	7 tablespoons red wine
rosemary sprigs to garnish	5 tablespoons tomato paste
	rosemary sprigs to garnish

Heat the oil in a flameproof casserole, add the garlic and rosemary and fry gently for 5 minutes until browned. Add the meat, spice(s) and salt and pepper to taste and fry until the meat is browned on all sides.

Add the wine and simmer until reduced slightly. Stir in the tomato purée (paste), dissolved in a little warm water. Simmer, stirring, for 3 minutes, then add enough water to cover the meat. Bring to the boil.

Cover the casserole, lower the heat and simmer for 2 hours or until the meat is tender, stirring occasionally and adding more water as necessary to cover the meat. Serve hot, garnished with rosemary.
SERVES 4

STUFATO DI MANZO

Beef Casseroled in White Wine

Metric/Imperial	American
25 g/1 oz lard	2 tablespoons lard
50 g/2 oz raw ham or bacon, chopped	¼ cup chopped raw ham or bacon
½ onion, peeled and chopped	½ onion, peeled and chopped
1 garlic clove, peeled and crushed	1 garlic clove, peeled and crushed
1 kg/2 lb stewing beef, sliced	2 lb stewing beef, sliced
pinch of dried marjoram	pinch of dried marjoram
salt and freshly ground black pepper	salt and freshly ground black pepper
7 tablespoons dry white wine	7 tablespoons dry white wine
2 tablespoons tomato purée	2 tablespoons tomato paste

Melt the lard in a flameproof casserole, add the ham or bacon, onion and garlic and fry gently until browned. Add the meat, marjoram and salt and pepper to taste and fry over moderate heat until the meat is browned on all sides.

Add the wine and simmer until reduced slightly. Stir in the tomato purée (paste), dissolved in a few tablespoons of water, and simmer for 3 minutes, stirring frequently. Pour in enough water to cover the meat and bring to the boil.

Cover the casserole, lower the heat and simmer for 2 hours or until the meat is tender, stirring occasionally and adding more water as necessary. Serve hot.
SERVES 4 TO 6

BISTECCHINE ALLA NAPOLETANA

Fillet Steak with Ham and Mushrooms

Metric/Imperial	American
3 tablespoons olive oil	3 tablespoons olive oil
100 g/4 oz prosciutto★ or raw smoked ham, chopped	½ cup chopped prosciutto★ or raw smoked ham
225 g/8 oz mushrooms, sliced	2½ cups sliced mushrooms
salt and freshly ground black pepper	salt and freshly ground black pepper
1 tablespoon chopped parsley	1 tablespoon chopped parsley
8 slices beef fillet, each weighing 50 g/2 oz	8 slices beef filet, each weighing 2 oz
juice of ½ lemon	juice of ½ lemon

Heat half the oil in a flameproof casserole, add the ham, mushrooms and salt and pepper to taste and sauté for 5 minutes. Sprinkle with the parsley.

Arrange the beef slices on top, without overlapping the slices. Sprinkle with a little salt, the lemon juice and the remaining oil. Cook in a preheated moderate oven (180°C/350°F/Gas Mark 4) for 20 minutes, turning the steaks and basting them with the cooking juices halfway through cooking. Serve immediately.
SERVES 4

RIGHT: Ossibuchi alla
milanese served with
Risotto alla milanese;
Costolette alla milanese

RUSTIN NEGAÀ
Veal Cutlets with Sage and Rosemary

Metric/Imperial	American
4 large veal cutlets	4 large veal cutlets
plain flour for coating	all-purpose flour for coating
50 g/2 oz butter	¼ cup butter
75 g/3 oz streaky bacon, diced	⅓ cup diced fatty bacon
salt and freshly ground black pepper	salt and freshly ground black pepper
4 sage leaves, chopped	4 sage leaves, chopped
1 teaspoon chopped rosemary	1 teaspoon chopped rosemary
300 ml/½ pint dry white wine	1¼ cups dry white wine
200 ml/⅓ pint beef stock	1 cup beef stock

Coat the veal with flour. Melt the butter in a frying pan
(skillet). Add the bacon and fry gently for 5 minutes.
Add the cutlets, sprinkle with salt and pepper and
brown on both sides.

Add the sage, rosemary and wine and simmer until
the wine has evaporated. Gradually stir in the stock,
lower the heat and simmer for 30 minutes.

Transfer the cutlets to a warmed serving dish; keep
hot. Boil the cooking juices until reduced and thickened, then pour over the meat. Serve hot with Risotto
alla milanese (see page 32) or mashed potatoes.
SERVES 4

ARROSTO DI VITELLO AL LATTE
Veal Cooked in Milk

Metric/Imperial	American
750 g/1¾ lb boned and rolled loin of veal	1¾ lb boned and rolled veal loin
75 g/3 oz lean bacon, cut into strips	⅓ cup lean bacon strips
salt and freshly ground black pepper	salt and freshly ground black pepper
plain flour for coating	all-purpose flour for coating
75 g/3 oz butter	⅓ cup butter
1 litre/1¾ pints milk (approximately)	4¼ cups milk (approximately)

Make deep incisions over the surface of the meat and
insert the strips of bacon. Sprinkle with salt and pepper
to taste, then coat lightly with flour.

Melt the butter in a flameproof casserole, add the
meat and fry, turning over moderate heat to brown on
all sides. Bring the milk to the boil and pour over the
meat. Lower the heat and simmer, uncovered, for 1½
hours or until the meat is tender, basting with the milk
from time to time.

Lift out the meat, slice and arrange on a serving
platter. Beat the milk remaining in the pan over low
heat for a few minutes until creamy. Pour over the meat
and serve immediately.
SERVES 4

OSSIBUCHI ALLA MILANESE
Braised Shin of Veal

*Ossibuchi are veal slices, about 5 cm/2 inches thick, cut
across the top of the leg. Each piece consists of a piece of bone
with marrow in the centre, surrounded by meat. You may
need to order ossibuchi in advance from your butcher.*

Metric/Imperial	American
4 ossibuchi	4 ossibuchi
plain flour for coating	all-purpose flour for coating
65 g/2½ oz butter	5 tablespoons butter
½ onion, peeled and chopped	½ onion, peeled and chopped
120 ml/4 fl oz dry white wine	1 cup dry white wine
350 g/12 oz tomatoes, peeled and diced	¾ lb tomatoes, peeled and diced
7 tablespoons stock	7 tablespoons stock
salt and freshly ground black pepper	salt and freshly ground black pepper
1 garlic clove, peeled and chopped	1 garlic clove, peeled and chopped
1 small bunch parsley, chopped	1 small bunch parsley, chopped
finely grated rind of ½ lemon	finely grated rind of ½ lemon

Coat the veal lightly with flour. Melt the butter in a
flameproof casserole, add the onion and fry gently for 5
minutes. Remove and set aside. Add the veal and fry
quickly to brown on both sides. Replace the onion.

Add the wine, tomatoes, stock and seasoning to taste.
Cover and simmer for 1¼ hours, basting occasionally.

Mix together the garlic, parsley and lemon rind and
sprinkle over the meat. Cook for a further 10 minutes.
Serve hot with Risotto alla milanese (see page 32).
SERVES 4

COSTOLETTE ALLA MILANESE
Milanese Veal Escalopes

Metric/Imperial	American
4 veal escalopes, each weighing 100 g/4 oz	4 veal scallopini, each weighing ¼ lb
1–2 eggs, beaten	1–2 eggs, beaten
dried breadcrumbs for coating	dried bread crumbs for coating
75 g/3 oz butter	⅓ cup butter
salt and freshly ground black pepper	salt and freshly ground black pepper
TO GARNISH:	TO GARNISH:
lemon twists	lemon twists
parsley sprigs	parsley sprigs

Beat the veal lightly with a mallet to flatten. Dip into
the beaten egg and coat with breadcrumbs.

Melt the butter in a large frying pan (skillet), and fry
the veal for 2 to 3 minutes on each side until tender and
golden brown. Transfer to a warmed serving dish and
sprinkle with salt and pepper to taste. Garnish with
lemon and parsley and serve immediately.
SERVES 4

*Ossibucchi alla milanese is
one of the great classic
Italian dishes. Strictly
speaking, it should be
made with the marrow
bones of tender young
veal – the marrow is
'dug' out of the centre of
each bone with a special
marrow spoon by the
diner. It is considered to
be a great delicacy by the
Milanese who created
this dish. The traditional
garnish of garlic, parsley
and grated lemon rind is
known as* gremolata *in
Milan, and no dish of*
ossibucchi *is complete
without it, nor its
saffron-coloured rice
accompaniment,* Risotto
alla milanese.

OLETTE ALLA BOLOGNESE

'eal Escalopes with Ham, Cheese and Tomatoes

Metric/Imperial	American
4 tablespoons olive oil	¼ cup olive oil
½ onion, peeled and chopped	½ onion, peeled and chopped
225 g/8 oz tomatoes, skinned and mashed	1 cup skinned and mashed tomatoes
salt and freshly ground black pepper	salt and freshly ground black pepper
4 veal escalopes, each weighing 100 g/4 oz	4 veal scallopini, each weighing ¼ lb
plain flour for coating	all-purpose flour for coating
2 eggs, beaten	2 eggs, beaten
dried breadcrumbs for coating	dried bread crumbs for coating
75 g/3 oz butter	⅓ cup butter
4 slices prosciutto★ or cooked ham	4 slices proscuitto★ or cooked ham
4 slices gruyère cheese	4 slices gruyère cheese

Heat the oil in a heavy pan, add the onion and fry gently for 5 minutes. Add the tomatoes and salt and pepper to taste, then cook gently for 20 minutes, stirring occasionally.

Meanwhile, beat the veal slices slightly, then coat lightly with flour. Dip into the beaten egg, then coat with breadcrumbs.

Melt two thirds of the butter in a large frying pan (skillet), add the veal and brown quickly on both sides. Transfer to a buttered ovenproof dish. Cover each piece of veal with a slice of ham and a slice of cheese. Sprinkle with a little salt and pepper.

Bake in a preheated moderately hot oven (190°C/375°F/Gas Mark 5) for 5 to 10 minutes or until the cheese has melted. Place the veal on a warmed serving platter, pour over the sauce and serve immediately.

SERVES 4

ARROSTO DI VITELLO RIPIENO

Veal Roll with Spinach

Metric/Imperial	American
2 eggs	2 eggs
75 g/3 oz Parmesan cheese★, grated	¾ cup grated Parmesan cheese★
salt and freshly ground black pepper	salt and freshly ground black pepper
100 g/4 oz butter	½ cup butter
450 g/1 lb cooked spinach, well drained and chopped	2 cups chopped cooked spinach, well drained
100 g/4 oz bacon rashers, derinded	6 bacon slices, derinded
750 g/1¾ lb slice leg of veal	1¾ lb slice leg of veal
3 tablespoons olive oil	3 tablespoons olive oil
120 ml/4 fl oz beef stock	½ cup beef stock
parsley sprigs to garnish	parsley sprigs to garnish

Put the eggs in a bowl with a third of the Parmesan and a pinch each of salt and pepper. Beat well to mix. Melt 1 tablespoon of the butter in a frying pan (skillet), add the egg mixture and fry on both sides to make an omelet. Remove from the pan and set aside.

Melt 1½ tablespoons butter in a heavy pan, add the remaining Parmesan and the spinach and cook, stirring, for a few minutes. Add salt and pepper to taste, remove from the heat and leave to cool.

Spread the bacon over the veal, cover with the omelet, then top with the spinach. Roll the veal around the stuffing, then sew or tie securely with thread or string.

Heat the oil and the remaining butter in a flame-proof casserole, add the veal roll and fry, turning until browned on all sides. Sprinkle with salt and pepper to taste and add the stock. Cover and simmer for 1½ hours or until the meat is tender, basting occasionally with the pan juices.

Remove the thread or string, then cut the veal into fairly thick slices. Serve hot, garnished with parsley.

SERVES 4

ABOVE: **Cotolette alla bolognese; Arrosto di vitello ripieno; Saltimbocca alla romana**

OSSIBUCHI ALLA REGGIANA

Roman Shin of Veal Casserole

Metric/Imperial	American
50 g/2 oz butter	¼ cup butter
1 small onion, peeled and finely chopped	1 small onion, peeled and finely chopped
1 garlic clove, peeled and crushed	1 garlic clove, peeled and crushed
4 ossibuchi (see page 52)	4 ossibuchi (see page 52)
pinch of ground mixed spice	pinch each of ground allspice and cinnamon
salt and freshly ground black pepper	salt and freshly ground black pepper
7 tablespoons dry Marsala wine	7 tablespoons dry Marsala wine
450 g/1 lb tomatoes, skinned and mashed	2 cups skinned and mashed tomatoes
Risotto alla parmigiana (see page 35), to serve	Risotto alla parmigiana (see page 35), to serve

Melt the butter in a flameproof casserole, add the onion and garlic and fry gently for 5 minutes. Add the veal, spice(s) and salt and pepper to taste and fry until the veal is browned on all sides.

Add the Marsala and simmer until evaporated. Add the tomatoes and enough hot water to cover the veal. Cover and simmer for 1½ hours until the veal is tender. Serve hot with the risotto.

SERVES 4

SALTIMBOCCA ALLA ROMANA

Veal and Ham Slices in Wine

Metric/Imperial	American
8 slices raw ham or bacon	8 slices raw ham or bacon
8 veal escalopes, each weighing 75 g/3 oz	8 veal scallopini, each weighing 3 oz
8–12 sage leaves	8–12 sage leaves
50 g/2 oz butter	¼ cup butter
7 tablespoons dry white wine	7 tablespoons dry white wine
salt and freshly ground black pepper	salt and freshly ground black pepper
sage leaves to garnish	sage leaves to garnish

Place a slice of ham on each slice of veal, then top with the sage leaves. Secure with cocktail sticks (toothpicks).

Melt the butter in a large frying pan (skillet), add the veal and fry until browned on both sides. Add the wine and salt and pepper to taste. Simmer for about 6 to 8 minutes until the meat is tender.

Transfer the saltimbocca to a warmed serving platter, removing the cocktail sticks (toothpicks). Add 1 tablespoon water to the pan and simmer, stirring, for 1 minute, then pour the pan juices over the saltimbocca. Garnish with sage and serve immediately.

SERVES 4

ABOVE: **Agnello al forno;**
Involtini al sugo
RIGHT: **Agnello imbottito**

INVOLTINI AL SUGO
Stuffed Veal Rolls in Tomato Sauce

Metric/Imperial

4 tablespoons olive oil
225 g/8 oz mushrooms,
  chopped
1 garlic clove, peeled and
  crushed
1 tablespoon chopped
  parsley
4–6 tablespoons beef stock
salt and freshly ground
  black pepper
225 g/8 oz cooked pork,
  minced
75 g/3 oz Parmesan
  cheese★, grated
1 egg, beaten
1 piece canned red pimento,
  chopped
8 veal escalopes, each
  weighing 50 g/2 oz
350 g/12 oz tomatoes,
  skinned and mashed

American

¼ cup olive oil
2½ cups chopped mushrooms
1 garlic clove, peeled and
  crushed
1 tablespoon chopped
  parsley
4–6 tablespoons beef stock
salt and freshly ground
  black pepper
1 cup ground cooked pork
¾ cup grated Parmesan
  cheese★
1 egg, beaten
1 piece canned red pimiento,
  chopped
8 veal scallopini, each
  weighing 2 oz
4½ cups skinned and mashed
  tomatoes

Heat half the oil in a flameproof casserole, add the mushrooms, garlic and parsley and cook gently for 15 minutes, adding a little of the stock to moisten if necessary. Add salt and pepper to taste, then transfer to a bowl. Add the pork, Parmesan, egg, pimento and a pinch of salt; stir well to mix.

Beat the veal with a mallet to flatten, then sprinkle lightly with salt and pepper and spread with the stuffing. Roll the veal around the stuffing and tie securely with string.

Heat the remaining oil in the casserole, add the veal rolls and fry over moderate heat for 5 minutes until browned on all sides. Add the tomatoes with salt and pepper to taste, then cover and cook gently for about 45 minutes until the meat is tender. Turn the meat during cooking and add a few tablespoons of stock to moisten if necessary.

Remove the meat from the casserole and untie the string. Arrange in a warmed serving dish and pour over the cooking juices. Serve immediately.
SERVES 4

ABBACCHIO ALLA ROMANA

Leg of Lamb Roman Style

Metric/Imperial	American
7 tablespoons olive oil	7 tablespoons olive oil
2 garlic cloves, peeled	2 garlic cloves, peeled
1 kg/2 lb leg of lamb	2 lb leg of lamb
salt and freshly ground black pepper	salt and freshly ground black pepper
1 rosemary sprig, chopped	1 rosemary sprig, chopped
2 canned anchovies, soaked in milk and drained	2 canned anchovies, soaked in milk and drained
3–4 tablespoons wine vinegar	3–4 tablespoons wine vinegar

Heat half the oil in a flameproof casserole, add 1 garlic clove and fry until browned. Remove the garlic, then add the meat to the casserole. Fry the meat over moderate heat, turning until browned on all sides. Sprinkle with salt and pepper to taste. Cover and cook in a preheated moderately hot oven (190°C/375°F/Gas Mark 5) for 1½ hours or until tender, basting and turning frequently.

Pound the rosemary, remaining garlic and the anchovies together using a mortar and pestle, then stir in the remaining oil and the vinegar. Transfer the meat to a warmed serving dish. Add the rosemary mixture to the casserole and simmer until reduced. Pour the juices over the meat and serve immediately.

SERVES 4

AGNELLO IMBOTTITO

Stuffed Breast of Lamb

Metric/Imperial	American
100 g/4 oz salami★, diced	½ cup diced salami★
100 g/4 oz provolone cheese★, diced	1 cup diced provolone cheese★
25 g/1 oz Parmesan cheese★, grated	¼ cup grated Parmesan cheese★
25 g/1 oz fresh breadcrumbs	½ cup fresh bread crumbs
25 g/1 oz parsley, chopped	¾ cup chopped parsley
salt and freshly ground black pepper	salt and freshly ground black pepper
1–2 eggs, beaten	1–2 eggs, beaten
1 kg/2 lb piece boned breast or shoulder of lamb	2 lb piece boned breast or shoulder of lamb
3–4 tablespoons olive oil	3–4 tablespoons olive oil
1 onion, peeled and chopped	1 onion, peeled and chopped
1 carrot, peeled and chopped	1 carrot, peeled and chopped
1 celery stick, chopped	1 celery stalk, chopped
1 garlic clove, peeled and crushed	1 garlic clove, peeled and crushed
150 ml/¼ pint dry white wine	⅔ cup dry white wine

Put the salami in a bowl with the cheeses, breadcrumbs, parsley and salt and pepper to taste. Stir well and mix in enough beaten egg to bind the stuffing. Leave to stand for 20 minutes.

Spread the mixture over the lamb and roll the meat around the stuffing. Tie securely with string. Heat the oil in a flameproof casserole, add the onion, carrot, celery and garlic, then place the meat on top. Sprinkle with salt and pepper to taste, then fry over moderate heat, turning the meat until it is browned on all sides.

Add the wine and 2 tablespoons water, then cover and cook gently for 1½ hours until the meat is tender, adding a little more water to moisten as necessary.

Remove the meat from the casserole, untie and cut into neat slices. Arrange the slices on a warmed serving platter. Strain the cooking juices and pour over the meat. Serve immediately.

SERVES 4

AGNELLO AL FORNO

Roast Lamb

Metric/Imperial	American
1 kg/2 lb leg of lamb	2 lb leg of lamb
100 g/4 oz lean bacon, chopped	½ cup chopped lean bacon
3 garlic cloves, peeled and slivered	3 garlic cloves, peeled and slivered
2 rosemary sprigs	2 rosemary sprigs
4 tablespoons olive oil	4 tablespoons olive oil
salt and freshly ground black pepper	salt and freshly ground black pepper

Make deep incisions in the meat and insert the bacon, garlic and rosemary leaves. Use half of the oil to grease a roasting pan and put the lamb into the pan.

Sprinkle with salt and pepper and the remaining oil. Roast in a preheated moderately hot oven (190°C/375°F/Gas Mark 5) for 1½ hours or until the meat is tender, basting occasionally. Transfer to a warmed serving dish and serve immediately.

SERVES 4

Agnello is the Italian word for lamb; *abbacchio* is a very special kind of lamb which is most often found in the region of Lazio. It is highly prized by the Romans, especially around Eastertime when whole baby lambs can be seen roasting on spits in the open air. *Abbacchio* is an unweaned lamb that has never eaten grass (like *vitello da latte*); it is therefore very tender with a sweet flavour. The Romans like to enhance this natural flavour by cooking it with fresh rosemary.

AGNELLO ALLA LUCANA

Leg of Lamb with Tomatoes

Metric/Imperial	American
50 g/2 oz lard	$\frac{1}{4}$ cup lard
1 kg/2 lb boned leg of lamb, cut into serving pieces	2 lb boned leg of lamb, cut into serving pieces
pinch of dried marjoram	pinch of dried marjoram
400 g/14 oz potatoes, peeled and diced	14 oz potatoes, peeled and diced
225 g/8 oz pickling onions, peeled	$\frac{1}{2}$ lb baby onions, peeled
225 g/8 oz tomatoes, skinned and chopped	1 cup skinned and chopped tomatoes
50 g/2 oz pecorino cheese★, grated	$\frac{1}{2}$ cup grated pecorino cheese★
750 ml/1$\frac{1}{4}$ pints chicken stock	3 cups chicken stock
salt and freshly ground black pepper	salt and freshly ground black pepper

Heat the lard in a flameproof casserole. Add the meat and fry, turning, until evenly browned. Add the remaining ingredients, with salt and pepper to taste. Cover and cook in a preheated moderately hot oven (190°C/375°F/Gas Mark 5) for 1 hour or until the meat is tender, stirring occasionally during cooking. Serve hot.

SERVES 4

AGNELLO COI FINOCCHIETTI

Lamb with Fennel and Tomatoes

Metric/Imperial	American
5 tablespoons olive oil	5 tablespoons olive oil
1kg/2 lb boned leg of lamb, cut into serving pieces	2 lb boned leg of lamb, cut into serving pieces
1 onion, peeled and chopped	1 onion, peeled and chopped
400 g/14 oz tomatoes, skinned and mashed	1$\frac{3}{4}$ cups skinned and mashed tomatoes
salt and freshly ground black pepper	salt and freshly ground black pepper
675 g/1$\frac{1}{2}$ lb fennel, quartered	1$\frac{1}{2}$ lb fennel, quartered

Heat the oil in a flameproof casserole, add the meat and fry over moderate heat until lightly browned on all sides. Stir in the onion and fry for a further 5 minutes, then add the tomatoes and salt and pepper to taste. Lower the heat, cover and simmer for 40 minutes, adding a little water if the casserole becomes too dry during cooking.

Cook the fennel in boiling salted water for 20 minutes. Drain and reserve 200 ml/$\frac{1}{3}$ pint/1 cup of the cooking liquid.

Add the fennel and the reserved cooking liquid to the casserole and continue cooking for about 20 minutes until the meat is tender; the casserole should be fairly dry. Serve hot.

SERVES 4

Spit-roasting whole baby lambs over charcoal is a fairly common cooking method throughout central and southern Italy. The Sardinians have a most unusual way of cooking lambs.

The whole ungutted animal is placed in a leaf-lined hole in the ground, which is packed with glowing embers. It is covered with soil, a fire is lit on top and the meat cooks slowly for several hours. The idea was developed long ago by sheep thieves as a means of cooking lambs without being seen. These days this method is reserved for feast days.

ABOVE: **Agnello coi finocchietti; Impanadas; Agnello alla lucana**

AGNELLO AL VERDETTO

Lamb Casserole with Peas

Metric/Imperial	American
4 tablespoons olive oil	$\frac{1}{4}$ cup olive oil
1 onion, peeled and sliced	1 onion, peeled and sliced
1 kg/2 lb boned shoulder of lamb, cut into serving pieces	2 lb boned shoulder of lamb, cut into serving pieces
200 ml/8 fl oz dry white wine	1 cup dry white wine
salt and freshly ground black pepper	salt and freshly ground black pepper
300 g/11 oz fresh or frozen peas	$2\frac{3}{4}$ cups fresh or frozen peas
3 eggs, beaten	3 eggs, beaten
50 g/2 oz pecorino cheese★, grated	$\frac{1}{2}$ cup grated pecorino cheese★
50 g/2 oz Parmesan cheese★, grated	$\frac{1}{2}$ cup grated Parmesan cheese★
1 tablespoon chopped parsley	1 tablespoon chopped parsley

Heat the oil in a flameproof casserole, add the onion and fry gently for 5 minutes. Add the meat and fry until browned on all sides, then add the wine, an equal quantity of water and salt and pepper to taste.

Cover and cook in a preheated moderate oven (180°C/350°F/Gas Mark 4) for 1 hour. Add the peas and continue cooking for a further 30 minutes or until the meat is tender.

Mix the eggs with the cheeses and parsley. Pour this mixture over the lamb and cook for 5 minutes over a low heat on top of the stove, without stirring. Serve immediately.

SERVES 4

IMPANADAS

Meat Pasties

Metric/Imperial	American
7 tablespoons olive oil	7 tablespoons olive oil
1 garlic clove, peeled and chopped	1 garlic clove, peeled and chopped
675 g/1½ lb minced lamb or pork	3 cups ground lamb or pork
2 tomatoes, skinned and chopped	2 tomatoes, skinned and chopped
1 tablespoon chopped parsley	1 tablespoon chopped parsley
pinch of saffron powder	pinch of saffron powder
salt and freshly ground black pepper	salt and freshly ground black pepper
275 g/10 oz wholewheat flour	2½ cups wholewheat flour
6 tablespoons water (approximately)	6 tablespoons water (approximately)

Heat 2 tablespoons of the oil in a heavy pan, add the garlic and fry gently until browned. Add the meat and tomatoes and cook, stirring, over low heat for 15 minutes.

Transfer the mixture to a bowl, then add the parsley, saffron and salt and pepper to taste. Mix well, then set aside to cool.

Mix the flour with the remaining oil and a pinch of salt, then mix in enough water to form a smooth dough. Knead well, then roll out to a thin sheet. Cut the dough into 8 circles, making 4 of them 2.5 cm/1 inch larger than the other four.

Place the 4 larger circles on a greased baking tray (cookie sheet). Divide the meat mixture between them, then brush the edges of the dough with a little water. Cover with the smaller circles of dough, press the edges together firmly to seal, then flute.

Bake in a preheated moderate oven (180°C/350°F/Gas Mark 4) for 30 minutes until well risen and golden brown. Serve hot or cold.

SERVES 4

Meat Dishes| 59

ARROSTO DI MAIALE AL LATTE
Pork Cooked in Milk

Metric/Imperial	American
1 kg/2 lb leg of pork	2 lb leg of pork
450 ml/¾ pint dry white wine	2 cups dry white wine
1 garlic clove, peeled and sliced	1 garlic clove, peeled and sliced
plain flour for coating	all-purpose flour for coating
50 g/2 oz butter	¼ cup butter
1 rosemary sprig, chopped	1 rosemary sprig, chopped
750 ml/1¼ pints milk	3 cups milk
salt and freshly ground black pepper	salt and freshly ground black pepper

Put the meat in a dish. Add the wine and garlic, then leave to marinate in the refrigerator for 2 days.

Drain the meat, dry thoroughly, then sprinkle lightly with flour. Melt the butter in a flameproof casserole, add the meat and rosemary and fry over moderate heat until browned on all sides. Add the milk and salt and pepper to taste, lower the heat, cover and simmer for 2 hours or until the meat is tender.

Transfer the meat to a warmed serving platter; keep hot. Boil the cooking liquor until reduced to a creamy consistency. Slice the meat and serve hot, with the sauce.

SERVES 4

POLENTA CON OSELETI SCAMPAI
Meat Kebabs with Polenta

Metric/Imperial	American
1.5 litres/2½ pints water	6¼ cups water
salt	salt
400 g/14 oz maize flour	3½ cups maize flour
225 g/8 oz lean veal, cut into 2 cm/¾ inch cubes	½ lb lean veal, cut into ¾ inch cubes
225 g/8 oz lean pork, cut into 2 cm/¾ inch cubes	½ lb lean pork, cut into ¾ inch cubes
100 g/4 oz calf's liver, cut into 2 cm/¾ inch cubes	¼ lb veal liver, cut into ¾ inch cubes
100 g/4 oz pig's liver, cut into 2 cm/¾ inch cubes	¼ lb pork liver, cut into ¾ inch cubes
100 g/4 oz streaky bacon or belly pork, cut into 2 cm/¾ inch cubes	¼ lb fatty bacon or pork belly, cut into ¾ inch cubes
12–16 sage leaves	12–16 sage leaves
4 tablespoons olive oil	¼ cup olive oil
freshly ground black pepper	freshly ground black pepper
7 tablespoons dry white wine	7 tablespoons dry white wine
3–4 tablespoons beef stock	3–4 tablespoons beef stock

Bring a large pan of salted water to the boil. Stir in the maize flour and cook, stirring frequently over low heat for about 40 minutes, until the polenta is smooth and thickened.

Meanwhile thread the meat onto skewers, alternating the different kinds and interspersing them with sage leaves. Place the skewers in a single layer in the grill (broiler) pan. Sprinkle with the oil and salt and pepper to taste.

Grill (broil) the meat under a preheated hot grill (broiler) for about 20 minutes, turning the skewers over from time to time.

Transfer the kebab skewers to a deep roasting tin (pan) into which they fit snugly. Add the wine and stock and roast in a preheated hot oven (220°C/425°F/ Gas Mark 7) for 20 minutes.

Spread the polenta in a warmed serving dish, then top with the skewers of meat. Sprinkle with the meat juices and serve immediately.

SERVES 4

BELOW: **Polenta con oseleti scampai; Braciole di maiale alla romagnola**

EMILIA-ROMAGNA

BRACIOLE DI MAIALE ALLA ROMAGNOLA

Pork Chops with Sage and Rosemary

Metric/Imperial	American
4 pork chops, trimmed	4 pork chops, trimmed
salt and freshly ground black pepper	salt and freshly ground black pepper
1 garlic clove, peeled and chopped	1 garlic clove, peeled and chopped
1 rosemary sprig, chopped	1 rosemary sprig, chopped
few sage leaves, chopped	few sage leaves, chopped
7 tablespoons dry white wine	7 tablespoons dry white wine

Sprinkle the chops with salt and pepper and place in an oiled baking tin (pan). Sprinkle with the garlic, rosemary and sage, then add the wine and enough water to just cover the chops.

Bake in a preheated moderately hot oven (200°C/400°F/Gas Mark 6) for about 30 minutes until tender. Transfer the chops to a warmed serving dish, pour over the cooking juices and serve immediately.
SERVES 4

TUSCANY

BRACIOLE DI MAIALE UBRIACHE

Pork Chops with Fennel Seeds

Metric/Imperial	American
4 pork chops, trimmed	4 pork chops, trimmed
salt and freshly ground black pepper	salt and freshly ground black pepper
2 tablespoons olive oil	2 tablespoons olive oil
1 garlic clove, peeled and chopped	1 garlic clove, peeled and chopped
1 tablespoon chopped parsley	1 tablespoon chopped parsley
pinch of fennel seeds	pinch of fennel seeds
7 tablespoons dry red wine	7 tablespoons dry red wine

Sprinkle the chops with salt and pepper. Heat the oil in a flameproof casserole, add the chops, garlic, parsley and fennel seeds and fry over brisk heat until the chops are browned on both sides. Pour in the wine. Lower the heat, cover and cook gently for about 30 minutes or until the meat is tender and the wine is reduced completely. Serve immediately.
SERVES 4

TUSCANY

ARISTA DI MAIALE ALLA FIORENTINA

Loin of Pork with Rosemary

Metric/Imperial	American
1.5 kg/3 lb boned and rolled pork loin	3 lb boneless pork top loin roast
1 garlic clove, peeled and finely chopped	1 garlic clove, peeled and finely chopped
1 rosemary sprig, finely chopped	1 rosemary sprig, finely chopped
salt and freshly ground black pepper	salt and freshly ground black pepper
2 tablespoons dripping	2 tablespoons drippings

Make deep incisions in the meat with a sharp knife. Mix the garlic with the rosemary, adding salt and pepper to taste. Insert this mixture into the incisions in the meat.

Place the dripping(s) and meat in a baking tin (pan) and bake in a preheated moderately hot oven (200°C/400°F/Gas Mark 6) for 30 minutes. Lower the heat to moderate (180°C/350°F/Gas Mark 4) and cook for a further 1½ hours, turning the meat and basting with the cooking juices occasionally.

Serve the meat sliced, hot or cold, with the cooking juices poured over.
SERVES 6

Meat Dishes/ 61

The Italians invariably use calf's (veal) tripe because it is more delicate in flavour and less coarse in texture than other tripe. This is also true of calf's (veal) liver, which is considered very much a delicacy in Italy. The tripe and liver from other animals may be substituted in Italian recipes calling for calf's (veal), but more care must be taken in the cooking if it is to be as good. Soaking in milk before cooking often helps tenderize offal (variety meats), especially liver.

FEGATO DI VITELLO ALLA VENEZIANA
Veal Liver Venetian Style

Metric/Imperial	American
3–4 tablespoons olive oil	3–4 tablespoons olive oil
25 g/1 oz butter	2 tablespoons butter
450 g/1 lb onions, peeled and sliced	1 lb onions, peeled and sliced
1 tablespoon chopped parsley	1 tablespoon chopped parsley
450 g/1 lb calf's liver, sliced	1 lb veal liver, sliced
4 tablespoons beef stock	¼ cup beef stock
salt and freshly ground black pepper	salt and freshly ground black pepper

Heat the oil and butter in a frying pan (skillet), add the onions and parsley, cover and cook gently for 20 to 30 minutes until softened.

Add the liver, increase the heat and stir in the stock. Cook for 5 minutes, then remove from the heat and add salt and pepper to taste. Serve immediately with grilled (broiled) slices of polenta (see page 31), or fried bread.

SERVES 4

ROGNONE ALLA BOLOGNESE
Kidneys Braised with Onion

Metric/Imperial	American
4 tablespoons olive oil	¼ cup olive oil
2 calf's kidneys, thinly sliced	2 veal kidneys, thinly sliced
3–4 tablespoons vinegar	3–4 tablespoons vinegar
50 g/2 oz butter	¼ cup butter
1 onion, peeled and finely chopped	1 onion, peeled and finely chopped
1 garlic clove, peeled	1 garlic clove, peeled
1 tablespoon chopped parsley	1 tablespoon chopped parsley
3–4 tablespoons beef stock	3–4 tablespoons beef stock
salt and freshly ground black pepper	salt and freshly ground black pepper

Heat the oil in a heavy pan, add the kidneys and fry gently for 4 to 5 minutes. Add half the vinegar and cook for a further 2 minutes, then drain the kidneys and keep hot.

Meanwhile, melt the butter in another pan. Add the onion, garlic and parsley and fry gently until browned. Discard the garlic and add the kidneys.

Increase the heat and cook, stirring, for a few minutes until the mixture is dry. Add the remaining vinegar and the stock and simmer for 5 minutes. Sprinkle with salt and pepper to taste and serve immediately.

SERVES 4

FRITTO MISTO ALLA ROMANA
Fried Kidneys and Sweetbreads, Roman-Style

Metric/Imperial	American
4 globe artichokes	4 globe artichokes
575 g/1¼ lb mixed lamb's offal (brains, kidneys, sweetbreads), cleaned and cut into serving pieces	1¼ lb mixed lamb's variety meats (brains, kidneys, sweetbreads), cleaned and cut into serving pieces
plain flour for coating	all-purpose flour for coating
2 eggs, beaten with a pinch of salt	2 eggs, beaten with a pinch of salt
vegetable oil for deep-frying	vegetable oil for deep-frying
salt and freshly ground black pepper	salt and freshly ground black pepper
2 lemons, quartered, to serve	2 lemons, quartered, to serve

Discard the hard outer leaves of the artichokes and the choke. Cut the hearts into sections. Coat the artichokes and meat with flour, then dip in the beaten eggs.

Heat the oil in a deep-fat fryer and deep-fry the different meats and artichokes separately until golden brown and cooked through. Drain on absorbent kitchen paper. Sprinkle with salt and pepper to taste and keep hot while cooking the remaining ingredients. Serve hot, with lemon quarters.

SERVES 4

TRIPPA ALLA BOLOGNESE

Tripe with Eggs and Parmesan

Metric/Imperial	American
1 kg/2 lb tripe, dressed and chopped	2 lb tripe, dressed and chopped
5 tablespoons olive oil	$\frac{1}{3}$ cup olive oil
100 g/4 oz bacon, chopped	$\frac{1}{2}$ cup chopped bacon
1 small onion, peeled and chopped	1 small onion, peeled and chopped
1 garlic clove, peeled and crushed	1 garlic clove, peeled and crushed
1 tablespoon chopped parsley	1 tablespoon chopped parsley
salt and freshly ground black pepper	salt and freshly ground black pepper
1 beef stock cube	1 beef bouillon cube
2 eggs, beaten	2 eggs, beaten
75 g/3 oz Parmesan cheese★, grated	$\frac{3}{4}$ cup grated Parmesan cheese★

Blanch the tripe in boiling water for 5 minutes, drain, then plunge into cold water.

Heat the oil in a heavy pan, add the bacon, onion, garlic and parsley and fry gently for 5 minutes. Add the tripe and salt and pepper to taste, then add the stock (bouillon) cube dissolved in a little warm water. Cook gently for 1 hour, stirring frequently.

Mix the eggs with half the Parmesan, stir into the tripe mixture and cook for a further 5 minutes. Transfer to a warmed serving dish, sprinkle with the remaining Parmesan and serve immediately.

SERVES 4

CODA ALLA VACCINARA

Oxtail Stew

Metric/Imperial	American
2 kg/4$\frac{1}{2}$ lb oxtail, cut into pieces	4$\frac{1}{2}$ lb oxtail, cut into pieces
2 onions, peeled	2 onions, peeled
2 carrots, peeled	2 carrots, peeled
575 g/1$\frac{1}{4}$ lb celery	1$\frac{1}{4}$ lb celery
2 bay leaves	2 bay leaves
salt	salt
1 tablespoon olive oil	1 tablespoon olive oil
225 g/8 oz lean bacon, chopped	1 cup chopped lean bacon
50 g/2 oz raw ham, chopped	$\frac{1}{4}$ cup chopped raw ham
7 tablespoons dry white wine	7 tablespoons dry white wine
450 g/1 lb tomatoes, skinned and mashed	2 cups skinned and mashed tomatoes
pinch of ground cinnamon	pinch of ground cinnamon
freshly ground black pepper	freshly ground black pepper

Soak the oxtail in cold water for 2 hours. Put 1 onion, 1 carrot, 1 celery stick and the bay leaves in a large pan of salted water and bring to the boil. Add the oxtail pieces

and bring to the boil. Boil for 1 hour, skimming frequently. Drain the oxtail, reserving the cooking liquid.

Chop the remaining onion and carrot. Heat the oil in a large clean pan, and add the onion, carrot, bacon, ham and oxtail. Fry, stirring, over moderate heat for 10 minutes, then add the wine and simmer until it has evaporated. Add the tomatoes, cover and simmer for 2$\frac{1}{2}$ hours, adding a little of the reserved cooking liquid from time to time as necessary.

Chop the remaining celery into 2 cm/$\frac{3}{4}$ inch long pieces. Cook in boiling salted water for 10 minutes, then drain and add to the oxtail. Cook for a further 30 minutes, then add the cinnamon and a little pepper. Serve hot.

SERVES 8

ABOVE: **Coda alla vaccinara; Rognone alla bolognese**
LEFT: **Fegato di vitello alla veneziana**

Poultry & Game

Poultry, in the form of capon, chicken, duck, goose and turkey, is popular throughout Italy, and is generally of good quality.

There are many different chicken specialities throughout the country, both using whole birds and chicken portions. Chicken breasts are cooked with ham, cheese or wine, or in a tomato sauce or devilled dressing (*alla diavola*). Whole chickens are often served roasted and stuffed, with the chicken livers and giblets included in homemade stuffings. Older birds or boiling fowl are usually simmered with herbs and seasonings, or made into soup or stock.

Turkey is popular in Italy, and is available throughout the year, both as whole birds and as thick turkey steaks or portions, which Italian housewives slice or cut up and use like veal, for escalope dishes or in stews. Turkeys are bred to huge sizes specifically for selling in portions in this way. Capon was always the traditional bird for Christmas, but nowadays turkey seems to be taking its place. The stuffing for either bird is likely to be made with breadcrumbs, minced pork, livers from the bird, herbs and seasonings, spicy sausage, fatty bacon and Parmesan. The stuffing is often moistened with Marsala. Another delicious recipe for roast turkey is *Tachinetta al melograno* (see page 67); it is served with a sauce of pomegranate juice.

There is a wide choice of game – both small birds and large game. The Italians do not impose rigid hunting and shooting restrictions so game is available most of the year. The Sardinians like to stuff large game with smaller game for celebration feasts and special occasions, then roast the animals and birds together over embers covered with myrtle leaves. In other regions of Italy game is cooked in a more conventional way – but very often in a sweet-sour (*agrodolce*) sauce, or marinated in wine and herbs. Rabbit is probably the most common game found in Italy, with hare another favourite, and both of these are often served with a sweet-sour sauce and slices of *polenta*.

TUSCANY

POLLO ALLO SPIEDO

Spit-Roasted Chicken

Metric/Imperial	American
1 × 1.5 kg/3 lb oven-ready chicken	1 × 3 lb oven-ready chicken
7 tablespoons olive oil	7 tablespoons olive oil
few sage leaves, chopped	few sage leaves, chopped
1 rosemary sprig, chopped	1 rosemary sprig, chopped
225 g/8 oz raw ham or bacon slices	½ lb raw ham or bacon slices
2 garlic cloves, peeled and chopped	2 garlic cloves, peeled and chopped
salt and freshly ground black pepper	salt and freshly ground black pepper

Brush the chicken with the oil, then sprinkle with half the sage and rosemary. Leave to stand for 2 to 3 hours.

Chop half the ham or bacon and mix with the garlic, remaining sage and rosemary, and salt and pepper to taste, then put inside the chicken. Sew the opening securely with trussing thread or string.

Wrap the chicken in the remaining slices of ham, then tie them on with more thread or string. Thread the chicken on the spit and spit roast for 1¼ hours until the skin is crunchy and the meat is tender. Alternatively, cook in a preheated moderately hot oven (200°C/400°F/Gas Mark 6) for 1¼ hours or until tender. Serve immediately.

SERVES 4

TUSCANY

POLLO ALLA DIAVOLA

Charcoal Grilled (Broiled) Chicken

Metric/Imperial	American
1 × 1.25 kg/2½ lb oven-ready chicken, halved	1 × 2½ lb oven-ready chicken, halved
7 tablespoons olive oil	7 tablespoons olive oil
salt and freshly ground black pepper	salt and freshly ground black pepper
1 lemon, sliced, to serve	1 lemon, sliced, to serve

Pound the 2 halves of chicken lightly with a mallet, taking care not to break the bones.

Rub the chicken halves with the oil and sprinkle with salt and pepper. Cook for about 40 minutes over a charcoal grill (broiler) until the skin is crisp and crunchy and the meat is tender.

Serve immediately, with lemon slices.

SERVES 4

POLLO IN POTACCHIO

Chicken Braised with Onion and Pimento

Metric/Imperial	American
3–4 tablespoons olive oil	3–4 tablespoons olive oil
1 small onion, peeled and sliced	1 small onion, peeled and sliced
2 garlic cloves, peeled and crushed	2 garlic cloves, peeled and crushed
1 × 1.25 kg/2½ lb oven-ready chicken, cut into serving pieces	1 × 2½ lb oven-ready chicken, cut into serving pieces
1 small piece canned pimento, chopped	1 small piece canned pimiento, chopped
salt and freshly ground black pepper	salt and freshly ground black pepper
1 tablespoon tomato purée	1 tablespoon tomato paste
3–4 tablespoons dry white wine	3–4 tablespoons dry white wine
few rosemary sprigs	few rosemary sprigs
6–8 tablespoons chicken stock	6–8 tablespoons chicken stock

Heat the oil in a flameproof casserole, add the onion and garlic and fry gently for 15 minutes. Add the chicken pieces with the pimento and salt and pepper to taste and fry, turning, over moderate heat until browned on all sides.

Mix the tomato purée (paste) with a little lukewarm water, then stir into the casserole with the wine. Lower the heat, cover and cook gently for 30 minutes. Chop one of the rosemary sprigs and sprinkle over the chicken. Cook for a further 30 minutes or until the chicken is tender, adding a little of the stock occasionally to moisten.

Serve hot, garnished with the remaining rosemary.

SERVES 4

ABOVE: **Pollo in potacchio**

The best chickens are said to come from Tuscany, specifically from the valley of the river Arno. They are noted for their plump tender flesh, which has an indescribably good flavour. The Tuscans rarely cook their chickens in elaborate sauces, for the simple reason that the birds are so good that this would only mar their flavour. Simple spit-roasting over a wood fire or charcoal grill (broiler) is the most favoured cooking method.

ABOVE: **Anatra farcita alla novarese; Gallina alla vernaccia**

POLLO RIPIENO AL FORNO

Roast Stuffed Chicken

Metric/Imperial
25 g/1 oz butter
1 × 1.5 kg/3 lb oven-ready chicken, with giblets
150 g/5 oz dried breadcrumbs
3 tomatoes, skinned and chopped
1 egg, beaten
100 g/4 oz pecorino cheese★, grated
7 tablespoons milk
4 tablespoons cream
salt and freshly ground black pepper
1 hard-boiled egg
4 tablespoons olive oil

American
2 tablespoons butter
1 × 3 lb oven-ready chicken, with giblets
1¼ cups dried bread crumbs
3 tomatoes, skinned and chopped
1 egg, beaten
1 cup grated pecorino cheese★
7 tablespoons milk
¼ cup cream
salt and freshly ground black pepper
1 hard-cooked egg
¼ cup olive oil

Melt the butter in a heavy pan, chop the chicken giblets and add to the pan. Fry gently for 10 minutes. Add the breadcrumbs and fry until browned, then add the tomatoes and simmer for 10 minutes. Remove from the heat and leave to cool.

Add the egg to the mixture with the cheese, milk, cream and salt and pepper to taste. Mix thoroughly. Stuff the chicken with this mixture, putting the hard-boiled (cooked) egg in the centre. Sew the opening securely with trussing thread or string.

Place the chicken in an oiled roasting tin (pan) and sprinkle with salt and pepper to taste and the oil. Roast in a preheated moderately hot oven (200°C/400°F/Gas Mark 6) for 1½ hours or until the chicken is tender. Serve immediately.

SERVES 6

GALLINA ALLA VERNACCIA

Chicken Casseroled with Garlic and White Wine

Metric/Imperial	American
4 tablespoons olive oil	¼ cup olive oil
3 garlic cloves, peeled	3 garlic cloves, peeled
1 × 1.5 kg/3 lb oven-ready chicken, cut into serving pieces	1 × 3 lb oven-ready chicken, cut into serving pieces
salt and freshly ground black pepper	salt and freshly ground black pepper
500 ml/18 fl oz Vernaccia or other dry white wine	2¼ cups Vernaccia or other dry white wine
chopped parsley to garnish	chopped parsley to garnish

Heat the oil in a flameproof casserole, add the garlic and fry gently until browned. Discard the garlic and add the chicken pieces to the casserole. Fry over high heat until browned on all sides, turning frequently. Add salt and pepper to taste, then add the wine.

Lower the heat, cover and cook gently for 1 hour or until the chicken is tender, stirring occasionally. Serve hot, garnished with parsley.

SERVES 6

TACCHINETTA AL MELOGRANO

Turkey with Pomegranates

Metric/Imperial	American
1 × 2 kg/4½ lb oven-ready turkey, with giblets	1 × 4½ lb oven-ready turkey, with giblets
salt	salt
50 g/2 oz butter, diced	¼ cup butter, diced
150 ml/¼ pint olive oil	⅔ cup olive oil
4 juniper berries	4 juniper berries
1 rosemary sprig	1 rosemary sprig
200 ml/⅓ pint dry white wine	1 cup dry white wine
3 pomegranates	3 pomegranates
freshly ground black pepper	freshly ground black pepper
juice of ½ lemon	juice of ½ lemon
4 tablespoons chicken stock	¼ cup chicken stock

Sprinkle the turkey inside and out with salt, then place a third of the butter in the cavity. Sew the opening with trussing thread or string.

Place the turkey in an oiled roasting tin (pan). Top with the remaining butter, 7 tablespoons oil, the juniper berries and rosemary, then pour in the wine. Roast in a preheated moderate oven (180°C/350°F/Gas Mark 4) for 1½ hours, basting the turkey with the wine and cooking juices occasionally. Add the juice of 1 pomegranate and cook for a further 1 hour or until the turkey is almost tender.

Meanwhile, chop the turkey liver and gizzard finely. Heat the remaining oil in a heavy pan, add the liver and gizzard and fry until browned. Remove from the heat and set aside.

Add the juice of another pomegranate and pepper to taste to the turkey. Roast for [...] minutes, then lift out the turkey and cut [...] pieces. Arrange in an ovenproof serving dish.

Skim the fat off the cooking juices and place the pan over moderate heat. Add the lemon juice and stock and boil until reduced by about half. Strain and stir into the giblet mixture. Pour this sauce over the turkey pieces, sprinkle with the grains of the remaining pomegranate and return to the oven for a further 7 to 8 minutes. Serve immediately.

SERVES 8

ANATRA FARCITA ALLA NOVARESE

Stuffed Duck Novara Style

Metric/Imperial	American
50 g/2 oz dripping	¼ cup drippings
50 g/2 oz bacon, chopped	¼ cup chopped bacon
1 onion, peeled and chopped	1 onion, peeled and chopped
225 g/8 oz minced beef	1 cup ground beef
225 g/8 oz minced pork	1 cup ground pork
100 g/4 oz salsiccia a metro★, skinned and diced	½ cup skinned and diced salsiccia a metro★
100 g/4 oz rice	scant ½ cup rice
salt	salt
3 eggs, beaten	3 eggs, beaten
1 garlic clove, peeled and crushed	1 garlic clove, peeled and crushed
1 tablespoon chopped parsley	1 tablespoon chopped parsley
pinch of grated nutmeg	pinch of grated nutmeg
freshly ground black pepper	freshly ground black pepper
1 × 1.5 kg/3½ lb oven-ready duckling, boned	1 × 3½ lb oven-ready duckling, boned
1–2 tablespoons olive oil	1–2 tablespoons olive oil
1 rosemary sprig	1 rosemary sprig
6–8 tablespoons chicken stock	6–8 tablespoons chicken stock

Melt the dripping(s) in a heavy pan, add the bacon and onion and fry gently for 5 minutes. Add the beef, pork and sausage and fry for 10 minutes, stirring frequently. Remove from the heat.

Cook the rice in boiling salted water for 10 minutes, then drain thoroughly and add to the meat mixture. Add the eggs, garlic, parsley, nutmeg and salt and pepper to taste and mix thoroughly.

Stuff the duckling with this mixture, then sew up with trussing thread or string. Heat the oil with the rosemary in a roasting tin (pan). Add the duck and brown on all sides, then roast in a preheated moderate oven (180°C/350°F/Gas Mark 4) for 1½ to 2 hours until the duck is tender, basting occasionally with a little stock. Slice the duck and serve hot, with the cooking juices poured over, or serve cold with salad.

SERVES 6

CONIGLIO CON LE OLIVE

Rabbit with Olives

Metric/Imperial	American
7 tablespoons olive oil	7 tablespoons olive oil
1 × 1.25 kg/2½ lb rabbit, cleaned and cut into serving pieces	1 × 2½ lb rabbit, cleaned and cut into serving pieces
2 garlic cloves, peeled and chopped	2 garlic cloves, peeled and chopped
1 rosemary sprig, chopped	1 rosemary sprig, chopped
200 ml/⅓ pint red wine	1 cup red wine
salt and freshly ground black pepper	salt and freshly ground black pepper
6–8 tablespoons chicken stock	6–8 tablespoons chicken stock
2 tomatoes, skinned and mashed	2 tomatoes, skinned and mashed
225 g/8 oz black olives, halved and stoned	1 cup pitted ripe olives

Heat the oil in a flameproof casserole, add the rabbit and sprinkle with the garlic and rosemary. Fry gently until the rabbit is browned on all sides, turning frequently.

Add the wine and salt and pepper to taste. Cover and simmer for 30 minutes, adding a little stock to moisten as necessary.

Add the tomatoes and olives and cook for a further 40 minutes until the rabbit is tender. Serve hot.

SERVES 4

CONIGLIO ALLA REGGIANA

Rabbit with Herbs

Metric/Imperial	American
1 × 1.25 kg/2½ lb rabbit, cleaned and cut into serving pieces	1 × 2½ lb rabbit, cleaned and cut into serving pieces
1 garlic clove, peeled and crushed	1 garlic clove, peeled and crushed
1 rosemary sprig, chopped	1 rosemary sprig, chopped
4 sage leaves, chopped	4 sage leaves, chopped
8 juniper berries	8 juniper berries
salt and freshly ground black pepper	salt and freshly ground black pepper
3–4 tablespoons vinegar	3–4 tablespoons vinegar
7 tablespoons olive oil	7 tablespoons olive oil
6–8 tablespoons chicken stock	6–8 tablespoons chicken stock

Put the rabbit in a flameproof casserole, sprinkle with the garlic, herbs, juniper, salt and pepper to taste, vinegar and two thirds of the oil. Leave to marinate for 3 to 4 hours, turning the rabbit pieces occasionally.

Add the remaining oil, then place the casserole on top of the stove. Cover and cook gently for 40 minutes, basting occasionally with the stock. Remove the lid, increase the heat to moderate and cook for a further 30 minutes until the rabbit is tender. Serve hot.

SERVES 4

CONIGLIO IN PORCHETTA

Rabbit and Fennel Casserole

Metric/Imperial	American
225 g/8 oz fennel (green part only), quartered	½ lb fennel (green part only), quartered
salt	salt
3 garlic cloves, peeled	3 garlic cloves, peeled
1 × 1.25 kg/2½ lb rabbit, cleaned, with liver	1 × 2½ lb rabbit, cleaned, with liver
100 g/4 oz bacon or raw ham	¼ lb bacon or raw ham
7 tablespoons olive oil	7 tablespoons olive oil
100 g/4 oz fresh breadcrumbs, soaked in a little milk and squeezed dry	2 cups fresh bread crumbs, soaked in a little milk and squeezed dry
freshly ground black pepper	freshly ground black pepper
fennel slices to garnish	fennel slices to garnish

Coniglio in porchetta;
Coniglio coi peperoni;
Coniglio con le olive

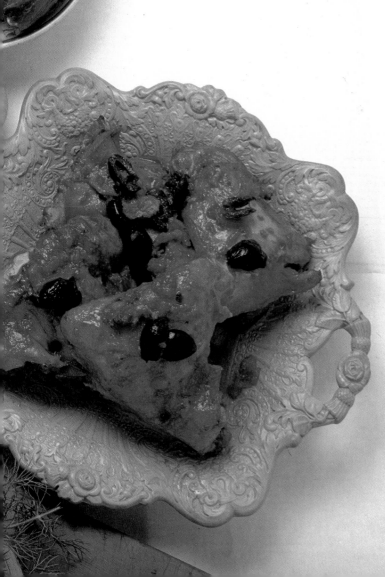

Cook the fennel in boiling salted water to cover, with 2 cloves garlic, for 15 minutes. Drain thoroughly, reserving the cooking liquid, but discarding the garlic. Chop the fennel finely.

Mince (grind) the liver together with the bacon and the remaining garlic. Heat 2 tablespoons oil in a flameproof casserole, add the fennel and liver mixture. Cook gently for 10 minutes, then mix with the breadcrumbs and salt and pepper to taste. Stuff the rabbit with this mixture, then sew up the opening with trussing thread or string.

Place the rabbit in a roasting tin (pan) and sprinkle with the remaining oil, and salt and pepper to taste. Cover with foil and roast in a preheated moderate oven (180°C/350°F/Gas Mark 4) for 1½ hours or until the rabbit is tender, basting occasionally with the fennel cooking liquid.

Transfer the rabbit to a serving platter and garnish with fennel. Serve hot.

SERVES 4

CONIGLIO COI PEPERONI

Rabbit with Peppers

Metric/Imperial	American
50 g/2 oz butter	¼ cup butter
50 g/2 oz ham fat or streaky bacon, chopped	¼ cup chopped ham fat or fatty bacon
1 rosemary sprig, chopped	1 rosemary sprig, chopped
1 × 1.25 kg/2½ lb rabbit, cleaned and cut into serving pieces	1 × 2½ lb rabbit, cleaned and cut into serving pieces
1 bay leaf	1 bay leaf
salt and freshly ground black pepper	salt and freshly ground black pepper
7 tablespoons chicken stock	7 tablespoons chicken stock
2 tablespoons olive oil	2 tablespoons olive oil
4 green peppers, cored, seeded and sliced	4 green peppers, cored, seeded and sliced
4 canned anchovies, soaked in milk, drained and mashed	4 canned anchovies, soaked in milk, drained and mashed
2 garlic cloves, peeled and sliced	2 garlic cloves, peeled and sliced
4 tablespoons white wine vinegar	¼ cup white wine vinegar

Melt half the butter in a flameproof casserole, add the ham fat or bacon and rosemary and fry gently for 5 minutes. Add the rabbit, bay leaf and salt and pepper to taste. Fry, turning over high heat until evenly browned, then cover and cook gently for 20 minutes, turning frequently and basting with the stock.

Meanwhile, heat the remaining butter and the oil in a separate pan. Add the peppers, anchovies, garlic and salt and pepper to taste. Cook gently for 20 minutes, adding the vinegar a little at a time during cooking.

Add the pepper mixture to the rabbit and cook gently for a further 30 minutes or until the rabbit is tender. Discard the bay leaf. Serve hot.

SERVES 4

FAGIANO COL RISOTTO

Pheasant with Risotto

Metric/Imperial	American
1 × 1.25 kg/2½ lb pheasant, cleaned	1 × 2½ lb pheasant, cleaned
salt	salt
4 streaky bacon rashers, derinded	4 fatty bacon slices
4 tablespoons olive oil	¼ cup olive oil
1 onion, peeled and chopped	1 onion, peeled and chopped
1 carrot, peeled and chopped	1 carrot, peeled and chopped
1 celery stick, chopped	1 celery stalk, chopped
1 bay leaf	1 bay leaf
chicken stock (see method)	chicken stock (see method)
RISOTTO:	RISOTTO:
50 g/2 oz butter	¼ cup butter
1 small onion, peeled and chopped	1 small onion, peeled and chopped
300 g/11 oz rice	1½ cups rice
3–4 tablespoons dry white wine	3–4 tablespoons dry white wine
1 litre/1¾ pints hot chicken stock	4¼ cups hot chicken stock
50 g/2 oz Parmesan cheese★, grated	½ cup grated Parmesan cheese★
freshly ground black pepper	freshly ground black pepper

Sprinkle the pheasant inside and out with salt, then wrap the bacon around the outside and secure with string.

Heat the oil in a flameproof casserole, add the chopped vegetables and the bay leaf and fry gently until lightly coloured. Add the pheasant and fry until browned on all sides, then lower the heat, cover and cook gently for 40 minutes until the pheasant is tender, adding a little stock from time to time to prevent sticking.

Meanwhile, make the risotto. Melt the butter in a heavy pan, add the onion and cook gently for 5 minutes. Add the rice and stir for 2 to 3 minutes over moderate heat, then add the wine and boil until reduced, stirring constantly. Continue cooking for 20 minutes, adding the stock a cupful at a time, as the liquid is absorbed.

Remove from the heat, stir in the Parmesan and salt and pepper to taste, then turn into a warmed serving dish. Remove the pheasant from the casserole and cut into serving pieces. Place on top of the risotto and spoon over the vegetables and cooking liquid. Serve immediately.

SERVES 4 TO 6

Without the gaming restrictions common to other European countries, the Italians are at liberty to shoot almost anything that flies whenever they want. Shooting is therefore a popular sport, and the smaller and rarer the bird, the greater delicacy it is. Among the birds that are shot for the tables are thrushes, larks, figpeckers, swallows, woodcock, snipe and blackbirds. The most popular cooking method for such birds is spit-roasting on skewers.

TORRESANI IN TECIA

Casseroled Pigeon with Peas

Metric/Imperial	American
4 tablespoons olive oil	4 tablespoons olive oil
100 g/4 oz lean bacon, diced	½ cup diced lean bacn
1 onion, peeled and chopped	1 onion, peeled and chopped
1 carrot, peeled and chopped	1 carrot, peeled and chopped
1 celery stick, chopped	1 celery stalk, chopped
1 garlic clove, peeled and chopped	1 garlic clove, peeled and chopped
4 young pigeons, cleaned and halved	4 young pigeons, cleaned and halved
7 tablespoons dry white wine	7 tablespoons dry white wine
350 g/12 oz shelled fresh peas	3 cups shelled fresh peas
pinch of ground cinnamon	pinch of ground cinnamon
salt and freshly ground black pepper	salt and freshly ground black pepper
450 ml/¾ pint chicken stock	2 cups chicken stock

Heat the oil in a flameproof casserole, add the bacon, vegetables and garlic, and fry gently for 10 minutes. Add the pigeons and fry until browned on all sides, turning frequently. Add the wine and cook until it has evaporated.

Add the peas, cinnamon, salt and pepper to taste, and the stock. Cover and simmer for 30 minutes or until the pigeons are tender, basting the pigeons with the cooking liquor occasionally. Serve hot.

SERVES 4

LEFT: **Fagiano arrosto;
Fagiano col risotto**
BELOW: **Torresani in tecia**

FAGIANO ARROSTO

Roast Pheasant with Sage

Metric/Imperial	American
100 g/4 oz raw ham, chopped	½ cup chopped raw ham
50 g/2 oz bacon, chopped	¼ cup chopped bacon
few sage leaves, chopped	few sage leaves, chopped
salt and freshly ground black pepper	salt and freshly ground black pepper
1 × 1.5 kg/3 lb pheasant, cleaned	1 × 3 lb pheasant, cleaned
4 bacon rashers	4 bacon slices
sage leaves to garnish	sage leaves to garnish

Mix the ham, bacon and sage together. Sprinkle the inside of the pheasant with salt and pepper, then fill with the ham mixture. Sew up the opening with trussing thread or string, then place the bacon on top and tie with string.

Place the pheasant in an oiled roasting tin (pan) and roast in a preheated moderately hot oven (190°C/375°F/Gas Mark 5) for 40 minutes until tender, basting occasionally with the pan juices.

Remove the thread or string from the pheasant and place on a warmed serving platter. Sprinkle with the cooking juices and garnish with sage leaves. Serve immediately.

SERVES 4

Vegetables

The Italians are blessed with an enormous variety of excellent vegetables, so it is hardly surprising to find that vegetables feature strongly in Italian cuisine. They may be included in soups or *antipasti*, or served as an accompaniment to a main course dish. Certain vegetables are often served as main courses in themselves.

Satisfying meals are made by stuffing artichokes, aubergines (eggplant), cabbage, peppers, onions, mushrooms or tomatoes, for example, with various mixtures of meat, cheese, rice, breadcrumbs, herbs and seasoning. Vegetables are also often served deep-fried, as *bignè* (fritters), or baked with cheese and other seasonings or sauces.

A popular, but unusual vegetable is the cardoon or *cardo*, an edible white thistle that is always served with *Bagna caôda* (see page 8). In their economical fashion, Italians cook the green leaves of beet and chard (turnip tops) in the same way as they cook spinach. One of the prettiest of Italian vegetables is *radicchio*, a type of chicory eaten as a salad vegetable, which varies in colour from bright red to pale pink, with fine white veins. Some varieties can be rather bitter-tasting, but they make a welcome alternative to lettuce in salads, and are well worth seeking out at Italian shops in the winter months.

Another highly prized vegetable (if *funghi* can be categorized as such) is the white truffle (*tartufo*). Italians are fortunate to be able to grow a large number of truffles, both black and white, but it is the latter of which they are particularly proud. Both kinds of truffle are used in cooking, especially as a garnish for dishes with veal escalopes, chicken and turkey breasts, and for risotto and pasta, in which case they are usually sliced raw onto the dish at the point of serving.

Italians eat an immense variety of mushrooms, or *funghi* as they should correctly be called. These are not the cultivated mushrooms so common in Great Britain and the United States, but wild mushrooms. The most popular mushroom in Italy is the *porcino*, a very tasty variety that makes cultivated mushrooms seem completely flavourless in comparison. After soaking they need very little cooking.

Tomatoes, peppers, courgettes (zucchini) and aubergines (eggplant) feature extensively in the cuisine of southern Italy. Italian tomatoes are always full of flavour whether they are the large deep-red ones, the oddly shaped green and yellow ones used raw in salads and *antipasto*, or the plum-shaped ones used for sauces, purées and general cooking purposes. In the summer months fresh tomatoes are used in practically everything. In winter Italians use canned ones, tomato sauce and purée (paste).

Pulses are frequently served as a vegetable accompaniment to meat in Italy rather than eaten as a separate dish. They are also used a great deal in soups.

ABOVE: **Cipolle farcite; Cuori di carciofi con spinaci**

CUORI DI CARCIOFI CON SPINACI

Artichoke Hearts with Spinach

Metric/Imperial	American
6 tablespoons olive oil	6 tablespoons olive oil
1 small onion, peeled and finely chopped	1 small onion, peeled and finely chopped
1 garlic clove, peeled and crushed	1 garlic clove, peeled and crushed
4 canned anchovies, drained and crushed	4 canned anchovies, drained and crushed
1 kg/2 lb spinach, washed, drained and finely chopped	2 lb spinach, washed, drained and finely chopped
25 g/1 oz plain flour	$\frac{1}{4}$ cup all-purpose flour
salt and freshly ground black pepper	salt and freshly ground black pepper
8 young globe artichokes	8 young globe artichokes
50 g/2 oz dried bread-crumbs	$\frac{1}{2}$ cup dried bread crumbs
50 g/2 oz Parmesan cheese★, grated	$\frac{1}{2}$ cup grated Parmesan cheese★

Heat half the oil in a large heavy pan. Add the onion, garlic and anchovies, and fry gently for 5 minutes. Add the spinach and cook for 2 minutes. Stir in the flour and salt and pepper to taste. Cover and cook gently for 5 minutes.

Clean the artichokes, discarding the hard outer leaves, spikes and chokes. Stand them close together in an oiled ovenproof dish, then cover with the spinach. Sprinkle with the remaining oil, breadcrumbs, cheese and pepper to taste. Bake in a preheated moderately hot oven (200°C/400°F/Gas Mark 6) for 20 minutes. Serve immediately.

SERVES 4 OR 8

Because the Italians serve vegetables more as complete dishes in their own right, than as mere accompaniments to meat, poultry or fish, vegetable recipes tend to be fairly involved. Stuffing vegetables is a very popular way of turning them into a substantial dish. Stuffed vegetables such as the ones on these pages are most likely to appear as first course dishes before the main course.

CIPOLLE FARCITE

Baked Stuffed Onions

Metric/Imperial	American
6 medium onions, peeled	6 medium onions, peeled
100 g/4 oz Parmesan cheese★, grated	1 cup grated Parmesan cheese★
75 g/3 oz butter	⅓ cup butter
3 eggs	3 eggs
salt and freshly ground black pepper	salt and freshly ground black pepper
3–4 tablespoons brandy	3–4 tablespoons brandy

Cook the onions in boiling water for 15 minutes. Drain, cut in half horizontally, then scoop out two thirds of the cores with a spoon. Chop the cores and place in a bowl with the cheese, one third of the butter, the eggs and salt and pepper to taste. Mix thoroughly, then spoon into the onion shells.

Melt the remaining butter in a flameproof casserole, put the onions in the dish and sprinkle with the brandy. Bake in a preheated moderately hot oven (200°C/400°F/Gas Mark 6) for 30 to 40 minutes. Serve immediately.

SERVES 6

PEPERONI RIPIENI DI RISO

Stuffed Peppers

Metric/Imperial	American
3 large green peppers	3 large green peppers
salt	salt
200 g/7 oz rice	1 cup rice
1 tablespoon chopped parsley	1 tablespoon chopped parsley
3 tablespoons olive oil	3 tablespoons olive oil
freshly ground black pepper	freshly ground black pepper
1 medium onion, peeled and sliced	1 medium onion, peeled and sliced
7 tablespoons dry white wine	7 tablespoons dry white wine

Halve the peppers lengthwise and remove the cores and seeds. Parboil the peppers in boiling salted water for 2 to 3 minutes, then drain and dry thoroughly. Cook the rice in boiling salted water for 10 minutes, then drain and mix with the parsley, 1 tablespoon oil and salt and pepper to taste.

Arrange the onion in an ovenproof dish. Fill the pepper halves with the rice mixture, then stand them upright on top of the onion. Sprinkle with the wine and the remaining oil, then cover and bake in a preheated moderately hot oven (200°C/400°F/Gas Mark 6) for 30 to 40 minutes. Serve hot or cold.

SERVES 6

FUNGHI AL FUNGHETTO

Mushrooms in Marjoram Sauce

Metric/Imperial	American
3 garlic cloves, peeled	3 garlic cloves, peeled
3–4 tablespoons olive oil ·	3–4 tablespoons olive oil
2 teaspoons chopped marjoram	2 teaspoons chopped marjoram
1 tablespoon tomato purée	1 tablespoon tomato paste
575 g/1½ lb mushrooms, sliced	1½ lb mushrooms, sliced
salt and freshly ground black pepper	salt and freshly ground black pepper

Chop 1 garlic clove. Heat the oil in a heavy pan, add the whole garlic cloves, chopped garlic, marjoram and tomato purée (paste) and fry gently for 5 minutes. Stir in the mushrooms and salt and pepper to taste. Simmer gently, stirring occasionally, for 15 minutes until just tender. Discard the whole garlic cloves and serve immediately.

SERVES 4 TO 6

FAGIOLI CON LE COTENNE

Bean, Bacon and Tomato Casserole

Metric/Imperial	American
200 g/7oz dried cannellini or haricot beans, soaked in lukewarm water overnight	1 cup dried cannellini or navy beans, soaked in lukewarm water overnight
1 rosemary sprig	1 rosemary sprig
3 garlic cloves, peeled	3 garlic cloves, peeled
½ lb streaky bacon, diced	½ lb fatty bacon, diced
½ onion, peeled and chopped	½ onion, peeled and chopped
1 small bunch parsley, chopped	1 small bunch parsley, chopped
4 basil leaves, chopped	4 basil leaves, chopped
2 tablespoons olive oil	2 tablespoons olive oil
450 g/1 lb tomatoes, skinned and chopped	2 cups skinned and chopped tomatoes
salt and freshly ground black pepper	salt and freshly ground black pepper

Drain the beans and place in a large pan with the rosemary and 2 whole garlic cloves. Cover with cold water and bring to the boil. Lower the heat, cover and simmer for 45 minutes to 1 hour until the beans are almost tender.

Meanwhile, chop the remaining garlic clove and mix with the bacon, onion, parsley and basil. Heat the oil in a flameproof casserole, add the mixture and fry gently until browned. Add the tomatoes and salt and pepper to taste. Cover and simmer gently for 30 minutes.

Drain the beans, discarding the garlic cloves and rosemary. Add the beans to the casserole and stir well. Cover and cook gently for a further 30 minutes. Adjust the seasoning and serve hot.

SERVES 4

CAVOLO ROSSO ALLA BOLZANESE

Red Cabbage Bolzano-Style

Metric/Imperial	American
75 g/3 oz smoked ham, diced	⅓ cup diced smoked ham
50 g/2 oz butter	¼ cup butter
3 tablespoons olive oil	3 tablespoons olive oil
½ onion, peeled and chopped	½ onion, peeled and chopped
7 tablespoons dry white wine	7 tablespoons dry white wine
1 large red cabbage, shredded	1 large red cabbage, shredded
salt and freshly ground black pepper	salt and freshly ground black pepper

Parboil the smoked ham in boiling water for 2 to 3 minutes, then drain and leave to cool.

Heat the butter and oil in a heavy pan, add the onion and ham and fry gently for 5 minutes. Add the wine and cabbage. Cover and simmer for 40 minutes, stirring occasionally. Add salt and pepper to taste before serving. Serve hot, with roast pork.

SERVES 4 TO 6

Liguria is renowned for its abundance of funghi. The Italians use every kind of edible funghi they can find, from the much coveted *funghi porcini*, to the somewhat strange-looking red, yellow and green varieties that are so common in the vegetable markets all over the country. *Funghi porcini* are often dried for winter use, so fond are the Italians of this variety.

The term *funghetti* can apply to any vegetable that has been cut into small pieces and fried with its skin on. It does not necessarily have to be mushrooms.

ASPARAGI ALLA MILANESE

Asparagus Milanese-Style

Metric/Imperial	American
1 kg/2 lb asparagus	2 lb asparagus
salt	salt
50 g/2 oz butter	¼ cup butter
4 eggs	4 eggs
freshly ground black pepper	freshly ground black pepper
50 g/2 oz Parmesan cheese★, grated	½ cup grated Parmesan cheese★

Scrape the lower part of the asparagus stems with a sharp knife, wash, then tie tightly together in small bundles. Stand the asparagus upright in a pan of boiling salted water so that the tips emerge just above water level. Cook for about 20 minutes or until the tips are soft to the touch, then drain, untie and place in individual warmed serving dishes; keep hot.

Heat half the butter in a large frying pan (skillet) until it turns brown. Break the eggs into the pan and sprinkle with salt and pepper to taste. Cook until the egg whites set slightly.

Using a spatula, remove the eggs and place them on top of the asparagus. Melt the remaining butter in the pan and sprinkle over the asparagus. Top with the Parmesan. Serve immediately.

SERVES 4

TORTA DI PATATE

Potato Cake

Metric/Imperial	American
575 g/1¼ lb potatoes, peeled	1¼ lb potatoes, peeled
125 g/4½ oz plain flour	1 cup plus 2 tablespoons all-purpose flour
salt and freshly ground black pepper	salt and freshly ground black pepper
3 eggs, beaten	3 eggs, beaten
4 tablespoons olive oil	¼ cup olive oil

Grate the potato into a bowl. Sift in the flour, with ¼ teaspoon salt and a pinch of pepper. Stir well, then mix in the eggs to form a soft, pliable dough.

Heat the oil in a frying pan (skillet), add the mixture and level it. Fry for about 7 minutes on each side until golden brown. Turn onto a warmed serving dish and serve immediately.

SERVES 6

ABOVE: **Funghi al funghetto; Asparagi alla milanese; Cavolo rosso alla bolzanese**

Vegetables/ 75

CAVOLFIORE FRITTO
Cauliflower Fritters

Metric/Imperial	American
100 g/4 oz plain flour	1 cup all-purpose flour
salt and freshly ground black pepper	salt and freshly ground black pepper
1 egg, beaten	1 egg, beaten
150 ml/¼ pint dry white wine (approximately)	⅔ cup dry white wine (approximately)
1 tablespoon aniseed liqueur (optional)	1 tablespoon aniseed liqueur (optional)
1 kg/2 lb cauliflower, divided into florets	2 lb cauliflower, divided into florets
vegetable oil for deep-frying	vegetable oil for deep-frying

Sift the flour with ¼ teaspoon salt and a pinch of pepper into a bowl, make a well in the centre, then add the egg and half the wine. Mix thoroughly, then stir in the aniseed liqueur, if using, and enough of the remaining wine to make a thick batter. Beat thoroughly, then cover and leave to stand for 1 hour.

Meanwhile, blanch the cauliflower in boiling salted water for 1 to 2 minutes. Drain and leave to cool.

Heat the oil in a deep-fat fryer. Dip the florets one at a time into the batter, then deep-fry a few at a time in the hot oil until golden brown. Drain on absorbent kitchen paper. Arrange on a warmed serving dish and sprinkle with salt. Serve immediately.

SERVES 4 TO 6

FAGIOLI ALL'UCCELLETTO
Broad (Lima) Beans in Tomato Sauce

Metric/Imperial	American
6 tablespoons olive oil	6 tablespoons olive oil
2 garlic cloves, peeled and chopped	2 garlic cloves, peeled and chopped
2 sage sprigs	2 sage sprigs
freshly ground black pepper	freshly ground black pepper
1 kg/2 lb fresh broad beans, shelled	2 lb fresh lima beans, shelled
salt	salt
350 g/12 oz tomatoes, skinned and chopped	1½ cups skinned and chopped tomatoes

Heat the oil in a flameproof casserole, add the garlic, sage and pepper to taste and fry gently for 5 minutes. Remove from the heat, add the beans and a pinch of salt and leave to stand for 3 to 4 minutes.

Add the tomatoes, cover and cook for 20 minutes or until the beans are tender, stirring occasionally. Remove the sage sprigs and serve immediately.

SERVES 4 TO 6

FAGIOLINI DI SANT'ANNA
French (Green) Beans in Garlic Sauce

Metric/Imperial	American
3 tablespoons olive oil	3 tablespoons olive oil
2 garlic cloves, peeled and crushed	2 garlic cloves, peeled and crushed
1 large ripe tomato, skinned and chopped	1 large ripe tomato, skinned and chopped
575 g/1¼ lb French beans, halved	1¼ lb green beans, halved
salt and freshly ground black pepper	salt and freshly ground black pepper

Heat the oil in a flameproof casserole, add the garlic and fry gently until browned. Stir in the tomato, then add the beans. Add enough water to barely cover the beans, then add salt and pepper to taste and bring to the boil. Lower the heat, cover and simmer for 20 to 25 minutes until the beans are tender. Remove the lid and increase the heat towards the end of the cooking time to reduce and thicken the liquor. Serve hot or cold.

SERVES 4

Carciofi alla guidea;
Spinaci alla romana;
Fagiolini di Sant'Anna

The Romans have the Jewish community in the city to thank for the pretty dish *Carciofi alla giudea*. In the Jewish quarter of Rome, this dish of deep-fried artichokes which look like roses is a speciality in many of the restaurants.

CARCIOFI ALLA GIUDEA

Fried Artichokes

Metric/Imperial	American
4 young globe artichokes	4 young globe artichokes
salt and freshly ground black pepper	salt and freshly ground black pepper
vegetable oil for shallow-frying	vegetable oil for shallow-frying

Remove the hard outer leaves, chokes and tips from the artichokes. Flatten the artichokes slightly by holding them upside down by their stems and pressing them against a work surface. Sprinkle the insides with salt and pepper.

Heat enough oil in a large frying pan (skillet) to cover the base of the pan, then place half the artichokes in the oil, stems downwards. Fry over moderate heat for 10 minutes, then turn over, increase the heat and fry for a further 10 minutes, turning frequently until golden brown and crunchy on all sides.

Drain the artichokes thoroughly on absorbent kitchen paper and keep hot while cooking the remainder. Serve immediately.

SERVES 4

SPINACI ALLA ROMANA

Spinach with Raisins and Pine Kernels

Metric/Imperial	American
1 kg/2 lb spinach	2 lb spinach
2 tablespoons olive oil	2 tablespoons olive oil
25 g/1 oz butter	2 tablespoons butter
1 garlic clove, peeled and sliced	1 garlic clove, peeled and sliced
25 g/1 oz pine kernels	$\frac{1}{4}$ cup pine kernels
25 g/1 oz seedless raisins, soaked in lukewarm water for 15 minutes and drained	$\frac{1}{3}$ cup seedless raisins, soaked in lukewarm water for 15 minutes and drained
salt and freshly ground black pepper	salt and freshly ground black pepper

Wash the spinach, then cook in a large pan, with only the water clinging to the leaves, until just tender. Drain well and squeeze out any excess water.

Heat the oil and butter in a heavy pan, add the garlic, fry gently until browned, then discard. Add the spinach to the pan with the pine kernels and raisins. Cook for 10 minutes, stirring frequently, then add salt and pepper to taste. Serve hot.

SERVES 4

Globe artichokes are one of the most popular vegetables in Italy, and they are readily available in most regions, although they are perhaps best liked in Lazio. Italian artichokes are usually very small and tender; some varieties are chokeless, so the whole artichoke can be eaten.

Many foods which we associate with France in fact originated in Italy. Petits pois, for instance, were brought to the court of Louis XIV from Genoa in the seventeenth century. They caused an immediate sensation and were considered a great luxury.

LAZIO

BROCCOLO STRASCINATO

Broccoli with Garlic

Metric/Imperial	American
1 kg/2 lb broccoli	2 lb broccoli
salt	salt
4 tablespoons olive oil	¼ cup olive oil
2 garlic cloves, peeled and sliced	2 garlic cloves, peeled and sliced
freshly ground black pepper	freshly ground black pepper

Cook the broccoli in boiling salted water for 15 minutes until almost tender. Drain and divide into florets.

Heat the oil in a heavy pan, add the garlic and fry gently until browned, then discard. Add the broccoli to the pan with salt and pepper to taste. Cook gently for 10 minutes, shaking the pan. Serve immediately.

SERVES 4 TO 6

LAZIO

FUNGHI ARROSTO ALLA ROMANA

Baked Mushrooms

Metric/Imperial	American
350 g/12 oz mushrooms, sliced	3 cups sliced mushrooms
salt and freshly ground black pepper	salt and freshly ground black pepper
1 tablespoon chopped parsley	1 tablespoon chopped parsley
1 garlic clove, peeled and crushed	1 garlic clove, peeled and crushed
2 tablespoons olive oil	2 tablespoons olive oil

Arrange the mushrooms in a single layer in an oiled ovenproof dish. Sprinkle with salt and pepper to taste, the parsley, garlic and oil. Bake in a preheated moderate oven (180°C/350°F/Gas Mark 4) for 20 minutes. Serve immediately.

SERVES 4

LAZIO

CARCIOFI COI PISELLI

Artichokes with Peas

Metric/Imperial	American
4 young globe artichokes	4 young globe artichokes
4 tablespoons olive oil	4 tablespoons olive oil
1 onion, peeled and finely chopped	1 onion, peeled and finely chopped
350 g/12 oz fresh shelled peas	¾ lb fresh shelled peas
75 g/3 oz raw ham or bacon, chopped	⅓ cup chopped raw ham or bacon
salt and freshly ground black pepper	salt and freshly ground black pepper
6–8 tablespoons chicken stock	6–8 tablespoons chicken stock

Remove the hard outer leaves and the chokes from the artichokes, then slice the artichokes lengthways.

Heat the oil in a large heavy pan, add the onion and fry gently for 5 minutes. Add the artichokes, cook for 15 minutes, then add the peas, ham and salt and pepper to taste. Stir in the stock and cook gently for 15 to 20 minutes, stirring occasionally, until the artichokes and peas are tender. Serve immediately.

SERVES 4

ABOVE: **Peperonata;**
Carciofi coi piselli
LEFT: **Funghi arrosto alla**
romana

LAZIO

PISELLI ALLA ROMANA COL PROSCIUTTO

Peas and Ham Roman-Style

Metric/Imperial
65 g/2½ oz butter
150 g/5 oz raw ham or
  bacon, with fat and lean
  chopped separately
1 onion, peeled and sliced
450 g/1 lb fresh shelled peas
7 tablespoons chicken stock
salt and freshly ground
  black pepper

American
5 tablespoons butter
5 oz raw ham or bacon,
  with fat and lean chopped
  separately
1 onion, peeled and sliced
1 lb fresh shelled peas
7 tablespoons chicken stock
salt and freshly ground
  black pepper

Melt half the butter in a heavy pan, add the ham or bacon fat and the onion and fry gently for 5 minutes. Add the peas, 2 tablespoons of the stock and a pinch each of salt and pepper. Cover and simmer for 10 minutes, stirring in the remaining stock a little at a time.

Stir in the remaining butter and the lean ham or bacon. Cook for a further 5 to 10 minutes until the peas are tender. Serve immediately.

SERVES 4

LAZIO

PEPERONATA

Peppers with Tomatoes and Onion

Metric/Imperial
6 tablespoons olive oil
1 onion, peeled and sliced
1 garlic clove, peeled and
  sliced
4 large fleshy green or red
  peppers, cored, seeded
  and sliced
salt and freshly ground
  black pepper
350 g/12 oz tomatoes,
  skinned and chopped
1 tablespoon chopped
  parsley

American
6 tablespoons olive oil
1 onion, peeled and sliced
1 garlic clove, peeled and
  sliced
4 large fleshy green or red
  peppers, cored, seeded
  and sliced
salt and freshly ground
  black pepper
1½ cups skinned and
  chopped tomatoes
1 tablespoon chopped
  parsley

Heat the oil in a heavy pan, add the onion and garlic and cook gently for 5 minutes. Add the peppers and salt and pepper to taste. Cook for a further 5 minutes, stirring occasionally.

Add the tomatoes and parsley. Adjust the seasoning, cover and simmer for 20 to 30 minutes, stirring frequently, until thickened. Serve hot or cold.

SERVES 4

MELANZANE RIPIENE
Stuffed Aubergines (Eggplants)

Metric/Imperial	American
4 small aubergines, cut in half lengthways	4 small eggplants, cut in half lengthways
2 tablespoons olive oil	2 tablespoons olive oil
1 onion, peeled and chopped	1 onion, peeled and chopped
225 g/8 oz tomatoes, skinned and chopped	1 cup skinned and chopped tomatoes
1 tablespoon chopped parsley	1 tablespoon chopped parsley
salt and freshly ground black pepper	salt and freshly ground black pepper
225 g/8 oz scamorza or mozzarella cheese★, sliced	½ lb scamorza or mozzarella cheese★, sliced
4 hard-boiled eggs, sliced	4 hard-cooked eggs, sliced
parsley sprigs to garnish	parsley sprigs to garnish

Scoop out the flesh of the aubergines (eggplants) with a spoon, leaving 1 cm/½ inch shells. Finely chop the flesh.

Heat the oil in a heavy pan, add the onion and fry gently for 5 minutes. Add the aubergine (eggplant) flesh, tomatoes, parsley and salt and pepper to taste. Stir well, then cook gently for 15 minutes.

Arrange the aubergine (eggplant) shells in an oiled shallow ovenproof dish and bake in a preheated moderate oven (180°C/350°F/Gas Mark 4) for 10 minutes. Spoon half the tomato mixture into the aubergine (eggplant) shells. Cover with alternate layers of cheese and egg slices. Spoon the remaining tomato mixture over the top, then return to the oven for a further 10 minutes. Serve hot or cold, garnished with parsley sprigs.
SERVES 4

MELANZANE A FUNGHETTI
Aubergines (Eggplants) with Tomato and Garlic Sauce

Metric/Imperial	American
2 large aubergines, cut into 2.5 cm/1 inch cubes	2 large eggplants, cut into 1 inch cubes
salt	salt
150 ml/¼ pint olive oil	⅔ cup olive oil
2 garlic cloves, peeled and crushed	2 garlic cloves, peeled and crushed
350 g/12 oz tomatoes, skinned and chopped	1½ cups skinned and chopped tomatoes
1 tablespoon capers	1 tablespoon capers
freshly ground black pepper	freshly ground black pepper

Put the aubergines (eggplants) in a colander, sprinkle lightly with salt and leave to stand for 1 hour.

Rinse the aubergines (eggplants) under cold running water, then drain and dry thoroughly. Heat the oil in a heavy pan, add the garlic and fry gently until browned. Add the aubergines (eggplants) and fry for 10 minutes, then add the tomatoes, capers and salt and pepper to taste. Cover and simmer for 30 to 40 minutes, stirring occasionally. Serve hot or cold.

SERVES 4

CARCIOFI RIPIENI
Stuffed Artichokes

Metric/Imperial	American
4 young globe artichokes	4 young globe artichokes
125 g/4½ oz canned tuna fish in oil, drained and mashed	4½ oz canned tuna fish in oil, drained and mashed
4 canned anchovies, drained and mashed	4 canned anchovies, drained and mashed
1 garlic clove, peeled and crushed	1 garlic clove, peeled and crushed
50 g/2 oz capers, mashed	¼ cup capers, mashed
1 tablespoon chopped parsley	1 tablespoon chopped parsley
salt and freshly ground black pepper	salt and freshly ground black pepper
6 tablespoons olive oil	6 tablespoons olive oil

Remove the hard outer leaves and chokes from the artichokes.

Mix the tuna with the anchovies, garlic, capers, parsley and salt and pepper to taste. Fill the centres of the artichokes with this mixture.

Place the artichokes very close together in a heavy pan and sprinkle with the oil. Add enough water to come halfway up the artichokes. Cover and cook for 30 minutes or until tender. Serve immediately.

SERVES 4

INSALATA DI RINFORZO
Cauliflower Salad

This is a Christmas salad which Italian housewives often add to (or 'reinforce') with new ingredients each day.

Metric/Imperial	American
1 cauliflower, divided into florets	1 cauliflower, divided into florets
salt	salt
50 g/2 oz green olives, halved and stoned	⅓ cup pitted green olives
50 g/2 oz black olives, halved and stoned	⅓ cup pitted ripe olives
50 g/2 oz pickled gherkins, sliced	⅓ cup sliced sweet dill pickles
50 g/2 oz pickled peppers, chopped	⅓ cup chopped pickled peppers
1 tablespoon capers	1 tablespoon capers
6 canned anchovies, drained	6 canned anchovies, drained
6 tablespoons olive oil	6 tablespoons olive oil
1 tablespoon vinegar	1 tablespoon vinegar
freshly ground black pepper	freshly ground black pepper

Cook the cauliflower in boiling salted water for 5 minutes; it should still be quite crisp. Drain and leave to cool.

Put the cauliflower in a bowl with the olives, gherkins (dill pickles), peppers, capers and anchovies. Add the oil, vinegar and salt and pepper to taste and fold gently to mix. Chill for at least 30 minutes before serving, to allow the flavours to mingle. Serve cold.

SERVES 4 TO 6

Carciofi ripiene; Insalata di rinforzo; Melanzane ripiene

ZUCCA ALL'AGRODOLCE

Sweet and Sour Pumpkin

Metric/Imperial	American
vegetable oil for shallow-frying	vegetable oil for shallow-frying
575 g/1¼ lb yellow pumpkin, skinned, seeded and thinly sliced	1¼ lb yellow pumpkin, skinned, seeded and thinly sliced
3–4 tablespoons wine vinegar	3–4 tablespoons wine vinegar
25 g/1 oz sugar	2 tablespoons sugar
1 tablespoon chopped mint	1 tablespoon chopped mint
2 garlic cloves, peeled and crushed	2 garlic cloves, peeled and crushed
salt and freshly ground black pepper	salt and freshly ground black pepper

Heat the oil to a depth of 5 mm/¼ inch in a large frying pan (skillet). Add the pumpkin slices and fry until golden brown on both sides. Drain off most of the oil from the pan, then add the vinegar, sugar, mint, garlic and salt and pepper to taste. Cook for a further 10 minutes, turning the pumpkin slices over halfway through cooking. Serve immediately.

SERVES 4

FUNGHI ALLA TRAPANESE

Mushrooms in Tomato and Wine Sauce

Metric/Imperial	American
450 g/1 lb mushrooms, sliced	5 cups sliced mushrooms
juice of 1 lemon	juice of 1 lemon
4 tablespoons olive oil	¼ cup olive oil
1 onion, peeled and chopped	1 onion, peeled and chopped
2 garlic cloves, peeled and crushed	2 garlic cloves, peeled and crushed
450 g/1 lb tomatoes, skinned, chopped and seeded	2 cups skinned, chopped and seeded tomatoes
salt and freshly ground black pepper	salt and freshly ground black pepper
7 tablespoons dry white wine	7 tablespoons dry white wine
chopped parsley to garnish	chopped parsley to garnish

Put the mushrooms in a bowl, sprinkle with the lemon juice and leave to stand.

Meanwhile, heat the oil in a heavy pan, add the onion and garlic and fry gently for 5 minutes. Add the tomatoes and simmer for 15 minutes, then add the mushrooms and salt and pepper to taste and simmer for a further 5 minutes.

Add the wine, increase the heat and boil until the wine has evaporated. Lower the heat and cook gently for about 10 minutes. Transfer to a warmed serving dish, sprinkle with parsley and serve immediately.

SERVES 4

ABOVE: **Carote in insalata;** **Caponata**

CAPONATA

Aubergines (Eggplants) with Tomatoes and Olives

Metric/Imperial	American
450 g/1 lb aubergines, diced	1 lb eggplants, diced
salt	salt
4 tablespoons vegetable oil	4 tablespoons vegetable oil
6 tablespoons olive oil	6 tablespoons olive oil
450 g/1 lb onions, peeled and finely chopped	1 lb onions, peeled and finely chopped
100 g/4 oz celery, parboiled and chopped	¼ lb celery, parboiled and chopped
150 g/5 oz green olives, halved and stoned	1 cup pitted green olives
450 g/1 lb tomatoes, skinned and mashed	2 cups skinned and mashed tomatoes
freshly ground black pepper	freshly ground black pepper
25 g/1 oz sugar	2 tablespoons sugar
7 tablespoons wine vinegar	7 tablespoons wine vinegar
2 tablespoons capers	2 tablespoons capers

CAROTE IN INSALATA

Carrot and Celery Salad

Metric/Imperial	American
1 head of celery, sliced	1 head of celery, sliced
450 g/1 lb young carrots, scrubbed and sliced diagonally	1 lb young carrots, scrubbed and sliced diagonally
3–4 tablespoons olive oil	3–4 tablespoons olive oil
juice of 1 lemon	juice of 1 lemon
1 tablespoon sugar	1 tablespoon sugar
salt and freshly ground black pepper	salt and freshly ground black pepper

Put the celery and carrots in a serving dish. Put the oil, lemon juice, sugar and a pinch each of salt and pepper in a screw-top jar and shake until thoroughly blended. Pour over the vegetables and toss well. Leave in a cool place for 1 hour before serving.
SERVES 6

FAGIOLI CON LE VERZE

Haricot (Navy) Beans and Cabbage

Metric/Imperial	American
350 g/12 oz dried haricot beans	1½ cups dried navy beans
2 pieces fennel, chopped	2 pieces fennel, chopped
1 onion, peeled and chopped	1 onion, peeled and chopped
1 green cabbage, shredded	1 green cabbage, shredded
4 tablespoons tomato purée	¼ cup tomato paste
salt and freshly ground black pepper	salt and freshly ground black pepper
2 tablespoons olive oil	2 tablespoons olive oil
100 g/4 oz streaky bacon, derinded and chopped	½ cup chopped fatty bacon
2 garlic cloves, peeled and crushed	2 garlic cloves, peeled and crushed

Soak the beans in lukewarm water overnight.

Drain the beans and place in a flameproof casserole. Cover with cold water and bring to the boil. Lower the heat, cover and simmer for 45 minutes, stirring occasionally.

Stir in the fennel, onion, cabbage, tomato purée (paste) and salt and pepper to taste and cook for a further 45 minutes or until the beans are tender.

Meanwhile, heat the oil in a small pan, add the bacon and garlic and fry until golden. Add to the casserole and cook for a further 5 minutes. Serve hot.
SERVES 6

Put the aubergines (eggplants) in a colander, sprinkle lightly with salt, then leave to stand for 1 hour.

Rinse the aubergines (eggplants) under cold running water, then drain and dry thoroughly. Heat the vegetable oil in a frying pan (skillet) and fry the aubergines (eggplants) until golden brown on all sides. Drain on absorbent kitchen paper.

Heat the olive oil in a heavy pan, add the onions and fry gently for 15 minutes. Add the celery, olives, tomatoes and a pinch each of salt and pepper. Cook for 5 minutes, then add the sugar, vinegar, capers and aubergines (eggplants). Cook for 10 minutes until the vinegar has evaporated.

Remove from the heat, adjust the seasoning and leave to cool. Serve cold.

SERVES 4

Vegetables in Italy are very often served as an *antipasto*, in which case they are usually either raw or only very lightly cooked and cooled. They are frequently tossed in a dressing of olive oil, lemon juice, herbs and seasonings. Globe artichokes, French (green) and broad (lima) beans, courgettes (zucchini), mushrooms, asparagus, fennel and carrots are among those served this way. Only freshly picked seasonal vegetables are used, when they are at the height of perfection. Italians rarely let any vegetable grow past its prime.

Desserts & Pâtisserie

Italians rarely finish a meal with a dessert; cheese and fresh fruit are normally served instead. They prefer to eat sweets, cakes and pastries at other times during the day. Possibly the only exceptions to this are *gelati* – ice creams, water ices and *granite* for which Italy is renowned. Many people say the Sicilians make the best ices, simply using fresh fruit purée and sugar for water ices, with eggs and cream added for ice cream.

Another area in which the Italians excel themselves is pastry-making. Italian pastry is rich but light, a combination that is difficult to achieve without some measure of skill and practice. For this reason, apart from on such special occasions as feast days, weddings and christenings, the Italian housewife buys most of her pastries from her local pâtisserie. Italian pastries contain delicious fillings; fresh and candied fruit, preserves, nuts, honey and ricotta cheese are most popular. *Cassata Siciliana*, the famous chilled desert cake, has layers of *ricotta* frozen with sponge, and there are even ices made from *ricotta* mixed with fruit and sugar.

Throughout Italy, special yeast cakes are eaten on festive days, including the famous *panettone* at Christmas and *colomba* at Easter. Biscuits (cookies) are popular too, particularly the almond macaroons from Turin, called *amaretti* (see page 86). There are many different kinds of *amaretti*, from the tiny button-shaped ones to *pinoccate* which are made with pine nuts.

Frittelle (sweet fritters with spice or fruit), *bignè* (fritters) and *bomboloni* (doughnuts – see page 88) are sold on street corners, especially on festival and carnival days.

PIEMONTE & VALLE D'AOSTA

CIAMBELLINE VALDOSTANE

Ring-shaped Biscuits (Cookies)

Metric/Imperial	American
450 g/1 lb fine maize flour	4 cups fine maize flour
50 g/2 oz plain flour	½ cup all-purpose flour
250 g/9 oz butter, cut into small pieces	1 cup plus 2 tablespoons butter, cut into small pieces
225 g/8 oz sugar	1¼ cups sugar
3 eggs, beaten	3 eggs, beaten
finely grated rind of ½ lemon	finely grated rind of ½ lemon

Mix the two flours together in a bowl and rub in the butter, using the fingertips. Add the sugar, eggs and lemon rind, then knead well together until smooth.

Put the mixture into a piping (pastry) bag, fitted with a 1 cm/½ inch plain nozzle, and pipe small rings onto a baking (cookie) sheet. Bake in a preheated moderate oven (180°C/350°F/Gas Mark 4) for 20 minutes or until golden. Leave on the sheets for 5 minutes, then transfer to a wire rack and cool completely.

MAKES 25 TO 30

PRUS MARTIN AL VINO

Pears Cooked in Wine

The Piedmontese most frequently use the locally produced Barolo wine for this dish, but it is equally good with medium white wine.

Metric/Imperial	American
750 g/1¾ lb firm cooking pears, peeled	1¾ lb firm cooking pears, peeled
450 ml/¾ pint medium red or white wine	2 cups medium red or white wine
100 g/4 oz sugar	½ cup sugar
4 whole cloves	4 whole cloves
pinch of ground cinnamon	pinch of ground cinnamon

Stand the pears in an ovenproof dish, pour over the wine, then sprinkle with the sugar, cloves and cinnamon.

Bake in a preheated moderate oven (160°C/325°F/Gas Mark 3) for 45 minutes or until the pears are tender and the liquor is thick and syrupy. Serve hot or cold.

SERVES 4 TO 6

PESCHE RIPIENE

Baked Stuffed Peaches

Metric/Imperial	American
4 ripe peaches, halved and stoned	4 ripe peaches, halved and pitted
4 blanched almonds, finely chopped	4 blanched almonds, finely chopped
8 macaroons, crushed	8 macaroons, crushed
75 g/3 oz sugar	⅓ cup sugar
25 g/1 oz cocoa powder	¼ cup unsweetened cocoa
7 tablespoons dry white wine	7 tablespoons dry white wine
40 g/1½ oz butter	3 tablespoons butter

Scoop out a little flesh from the hollows in the peaches and reserve. Mix together the almonds, macaroons, half the sugar, the cocoa, 1 tablespoon wine and the reserved peach flesh. Fill the peach halves with the mixture and top each one with a small piece of butter.

Arrange the peach halves in a buttered ovenproof dish, pour over the remaining wine and sprinkle with the remaining sugar. Bake in a preheated moderate oven (180°C/350°F/Gas Mark 4) for 25 to 30 minutes until the peaches are tender. Serve hot.

SERVES 4

Desserts and puddings as we know them figure rarely at the end of Italian meals, and recipes for these are not usual. The few Italian desserts listed under 'I Dolci' on Italian restaurant menus are probably there to pay a kind of lip-service to those of us who are used to a dessert course at the end of a meal. These desserts usually include a selection of rich and rather heavily decorated gâteaux, and it is rare to see an Italian choosing from this section of a menu. Most Italians prefer to end a meal with cheese or fresh fruit.

AMARETTI

Macaroons

If bitter almonds are not available, use all blanched almonds instead and decrease the amount of sugar by 2 tablespoons.

Metric/Imperial	American
225 g/8 oz blanched almonds	2 cups blanched almonds
50–75 g/2–3 oz bitter almonds	1 cup bitter almonds
350 g/12 oz caster sugar	1½ cups superfine sugar
25 g/1 oz plain flour, sifted	¼ cup all-purpose flour, sifted
4 egg whites	4 egg whites
few drops of vanilla essence	few drops of vanilla extract
¼ teaspoon grated lemon rind	¼ teaspoon grated lemon rind

Grind all the almonds together, using a pestle and mortar.

Place in a bowl with all except 2 tablespoons of the sugar and the flour; stir well to mix. Lightly whisk the egg whites with a fork, then add the vanilla and lemon rind. Add to the almond mixture gradually, until a smooth soft mixture, which holds its shape, is obtained.

Place small spoonfuls of the mixture on a greased and floured baking (cookie) sheet, spacing them well apart. Sprinkle with the remaining sugar and bake in a preheated moderate oven (180°C/350°F/Gas Mark 4) for about 20 minutes or until lightly browned. Transfer to a wire rack to cool completely before serving.

MAKES 35 TO 40

CRUMIRI

Crescent-shaped Biscuits (Cookies)

Metric/Imperial	American
250 g/9 oz fine maize flour	2¼ cups fine maize flour
200 g/7 oz coarse bran flour	1¾ cups coarse bran flour
275 g/10 oz butter, softened and cut into small pieces	1¼ cups butter, softened and cut into small pieces
175 g/6 oz sugar	¾ cup sugar
4 egg yolks	4 egg yolks
2 tablespoons honey	2 tablespoons honey
¼ teaspoon grated lemon rind	¼ teaspoon grated lemon rind

Mix the two flours together on a work surface and make a well in the centre. Add the remaining ingredients and work together, using the fingertips, to give a smooth, firm dough. Form into a ball, cover and chill for 30 minutes.

Put some of the mixture into a piping (pastry) bag, fitted with a 1 cm/½ inch plain nozzle, and pipe 7.5cm/3 inch long pieces onto a baking (cookie) sheet lined with greased greaseproof (wax) paper. Bend the pieces gently into crescent shapes. Repeat with the remaining mixture. Bake in a preheated moderate oven (160°C/325°F/Gas Mark 3) for 15 to 20 minutes until golden brown. Transfer to a wire rack to cool before serving.

MAKES 30 TO 35

BACI DI DAMA

Orange Almond Cookies

Metric/Imperial	American
100 g/4 oz blanched almonds, ground	1 cup ground blanched almonds
100 g/4 oz sugar	½ cup sugar
100 g/4 oz candied orange peel, minced	½ cup minced candied orange peel
100 g/4 oz plain flour, sifted	1 cup all-purpose flour, sifted
6–8 tablespoons milk	6–8 tablespoons milk
50 g/2 oz plain chocolate, melted	⅓ cup semi-sweet chocolate pieces, melted

Put the ground almonds in a bowl with the sugar, orange peel and all but 1 tablespoon of the flour. Mix well, then stir in enough milk to give a smooth, firm dough.

Roll into small balls and place, well apart, on a baking (cookie) sheet lined with greased greaseproof (wax) paper. Sprinkle with the remaining flour, and bake in a preheated moderate oven (180°C/350°F/Gas Mark 4) for 15 minutes or until golden brown.

Transfer to a wire rack to cool. When cold, sandwich the biscuits (cookies) together in pairs with the melted chocolate. Chill in the refrigerator for 1 hour before serving.

MAKES 12 TO 15

BICCIOLANI

Spiced Biscuits (Cookies)

Metric/Imperial	American
575 g/1¼ lb plain flour	5 cups all-purpose flour
200 g/7 oz sugar	1 cup sugar
1 tablespoon ground cinnamon	1 tablespoon ground cinnamon
20 coriander seeds	20 coriander seeds
pinch of salt	pinch of salt
pinch of grated nutmeg	pinch of grated nutmeg
5 whole cloves, ground	5 whole cloves, ground
350 g/12 oz butter, softened and cut into small pieces	1½ cups butter, softened and cut into small pieces
5 egg yolks	5 egg yolks

Sift the flour onto a work surface and mix in the sugar, cinnamon, coriander seeds, salt, nutmeg and cloves. Make a well in the centre, add the butter and egg yolks and work the ingredients together with the fingertips. Knead well together until smooth and quite soft. Cover and chill in the refrigerator for 3 hours.

Put some of the mixture in a piping (pastry) bag, fitted with a large plain nozzle, and pipe long 'ribbons' onto a baking (cookie) sheet lined with greased greaseproof (wax) paper. Repeat with the remaining mixture.

Bake in a preheated moderate oven (160°C/325°F/Gas Mark 3) for 15 to 20 minutes until golden brown. Cut into 9 cm/3½ inch lengths and transfer to a wire rack to cool before serving.

MAKES 30 TO 40

RIGHT: **Baci di dama; Amaretti; Bicciolani; Crumiri**

The Italians, renowned for their sweet tooths, have been fond of biscuits (cookies) for centuries – sugar was first brought to Europe via the Venetian traders. Pastry shop windows are full of different varieties, many of which are purely local to the area in which they are made. These are eaten at odd times in Italian homes – always offered to visitors with a glass of wine, no matter what time of the day they call. *Amaretti* are even eaten with aperitifs before a meal.

Nearly every region in Italy seems to have its own version of a celebration cake, although these have a texture and flavour more like sweetened bread than cake. They are eaten throughout the year with a cup of coffee or maybe dunked in a glass of wine (they are rather dry), but on feast days and other special occasions they appear in the shops in profusion. *Panettone* appears in Milan at Christmas, *Colomba* at Easter. *Pandoro* is a New Year speciality cake from Verona.

BUCCELLATO
Sweet Yeast Ring Cake

Metric/Imperial	American
400 g/14 oz plain flour	3½ cups all-purpose flour
200 g/7 oz caster sugar	1 cup sugar
2 eggs, beaten	2 eggs, beaten
100 g/4 oz butter, softened and cut into small pieces	½ cup butter, softened and cut into small pieces
2 teaspoons bicarbonate of soda	2 teaspoons baking soda
2 teaspoons dried yeast, dissolved in 2 tablespoons lukewarm milk	2 teaspoons active dry yeast, dissolved in 2 tablespoons lukewarm milk
pinch of salt	pinch of salt
few tablespoons warm milk to mix	few tablespoons warm milk to mix
beaten egg to glaze	beaten egg to glaze

Sift the flour into a bowl, stir in the sugar and make a well in the centre. Add the eggs, butter, soda, yeast and salt. Knead ingredients together, adding enough milk to form a soft dough. Knead well until smooth and pliable, shape into a ball, place in a bowl and cover with a damp cloth. Leave to rise in a warm place for 1 hour or until doubled in bulk.

Knead the dough on a work surface, then shape into a ring with your hands. Place on a baking (cookie) sheet lined with greased greaseproof (wax) paper. Brush with beaten egg. Bake in a preheated moderately hot oven (200°C/400°F/Gas Mark 6) for 40 minutes until risen and firm to the touch. Transfer to a wire rack to cool before serving.

SERVES 4 TO 6

PANFORTE DI SIENA
Siena Cake

This flat 'cake' with a nougat-like texture, rich in candied peel, toasted nuts and spices, is a particular speciality of the town of Siena.

Metric/Imperial	American
75 g/3 oz hazelnuts	½ cup filberts
75 g/3 oz blanched almonds, coarsely chopped	½ cup coarsely chopped blanched almonds
175 g/6 oz candied peel, finely chopped	1 cup finely chopped candied peel
25 g/1 oz cocoa powder	¼ cup unsweetened cocoa powder
50 g/2 oz plain flour	½ cup all-purpose flour
½ teaspoon ground cinnamon	½ teaspoon ground cinnamon
¼ teaspoon ground mixed spice	¼ teaspoon grated nutmeg
100 g/4 oz sugar	½ cup sugar
100 g/4 oz honey	½ cup honey
TOPPING:	TOPPING:
2 tablespoons icing sugar	2 tablespoons confectioners' sugar
1 teaspoon ground cinnamon	1 teaspoon ground cinnamon

Spread the hazelnuts (filberts) on a baking (cookie) sheet and put into a preheated moderately hot oven (190°C/375°F/Gas Mark 5) for 5 to 10 minutes. Rub the nuts in a clean cloth (napkin) to remove skins, then chop coarsely.

Place in a bowl with the almonds, candied peel, cocoa, flour and spices. Stir well.

Put the sugar and honey in a pan and heat gently until the sugar dissolves, then boil until a sugar thermometer registers 115°C/240°F, or until a little of the mixture dropped into a cup of cold water forms a ball. Take off the heat immediately, add to the nut mixture and stir until well mixed.

Turn into a 20 cm/8 inch flan ring (pie pan) lined with non-stick parchment. Spread flat, making sure the mixture is no more than 1 cm/½ inch thick. Bake in a preheated cool oven (150°C/300°F/Gas Mark 2) for 30 to 35 minutes.

Turn onto a wire rack, peel off the paper and leave to cool. Sprinkle the top thickly with the icing (confectioners') sugar sifted with the cinnamon. Serve cut into small wedges.

MAKES 8 TO 10 WEDGES

BOMBOLONI
Doughnuts

Metric/Imperial	American
450 g/1 lb plain flour	4 cups all-purpose flour
175 g/6 oz caster sugar	¾ cup sugar
finely grated rind of 1 lemon	finely grated rind of 1 lemon
pinch of salt	pinch of salt
75 g/3 oz butter, softened and cut into small pieces	⅓ cup butter, softened and cut into small pieces
15 g/½ oz fresh yeast, dissolved in 2 tablespoons warm water	½ cake compressed yeast, dissolved in 2 tablespoons warm water
vegetable oil for deep-frying	vegetable oil for deep-frying

Sift the flour into a bowl and stir in 75 g/3 oz/⅓ cup sugar, the lemon rind and salt. Make a well in the centre and add the butter and yeast. Mix the ingredients together, adding a little lukewarm water to form a soft dough. Knead well until smooth and pliable, shape into a ball and cover with a damp cloth. Leave to rise in a warm place for 1 hour or until doubled in bulk.

Flatten the dough with a rolling pin and roll out into a sheet about 1 cm/½ inch thick. Cut into circles, about 5 cm/2 inches in diameter, using a pastry (cookie) cutter. Place on a baking (cookie) sheet and leave to rise in a warm place for 1 hour.

Heat the oil in a deep-fryer and deep-fry the doughnuts a few at a time until golden brown. Drain on absorbent kitchen paper while frying the remainder. Sprinkle with the remaining sugar and serve immediately.

MAKES 15 TO 20

ABOVE: **Panforte di siena**

PINOCCATE
Pine Nut Candies

Metric/Imperial	American
150 g/5 oz candied orange peel, chopped	scant 1 cup chopped candied orange peel
7 tablespoons Maraschino liqueur	7 tablespoons Maraschino liqueur
200 ml/7 fl oz water	1 cup water
450 g/1 lb sugar	2 cups sugar
150 g/5 oz pine kernels	1⅓ cups pine kernels

Soak the orange peel in the liqueur.

Put the water and sugar in a pan over low heat until dissolved, then boil rapidly until the syrup thickens and reaches the 'thread' stage. To test, place a teaspoonful of the syrup in a cup of cold water to cool slightly, then draw the syrup between the thumb and forefinger. If it forms a thread the syrup is ready.

Remove from the heat and stir vigorously with a wooden spatula until white and soft. Drain the orange peel, then immediately add to the sugar with the pine kernels. Spoon small heaps of the mixture onto a sheet of buttered foil and leave to cool before serving.

MAKES 20 TO 25

GELATO DI RICOTTA
Ricotta and Rum Bombe

Metric/Imperial	American
5 egg yolks	5 egg yolks
100 g/4 oz sugar	½ cup sugar
5 tablespoons rum	⅓ cup rum
450 g/1 lb fresh ricotta cheese★, sieved	2 cups fresh ricotta cheese★, sieved

Line a 1.2 litre/2 pint freezerproof mould with foil.

Put the egg yolks in a bowl with the sugar and whisk until light and fluffy. Fold in the rum, then fold in the ricotta a little at a time.

Spoon the mixture into the prepared mould, smooth the surface, then cover with foil. Freeze until solid. Unmould onto a serving plate and serve immediately.

SERVES 4 TO 6

ABOVE: **Ricotta fritta;
Nepitelle**

NEPITELLE

Fig and Nut Pasties

Metric/Imperial

PASTRY:
400 g/14 oz plain flour
150 g/5 oz caster sugar
*165 g/5½ oz butter, softened
and cut into small pieces*
3 eggs
1 egg, separated
pinch of salt

FILLING:
300 g/11 oz dried figs
*150 g/5 oz shelled walnuts,
ground*
*150 g/5 oz blanched
almonds, toasted and
ground*
*100 g/4 oz seedless raisins,
soaked in lukewarm
water for 15 minutes and
drained*
200 g/7 oz marmalade
*finely grated rind of 3
oranges*
¼ teaspoon ground cloves
1 teaspoon ground cinnamon

American

PASTRY:
3½ cups all-purpose flour
⅔ cup sugar
*⅔ cup butter, softened and
cut into small pieces*
3 eggs
1 egg, separated
pinch of salt

FILLING:
2 cups dried figs
*1¼ cups shelled walnuts,
ground*
*1¼ cups blanched almonds,
toasted and ground*
*⅔ cup seedless raisins,
soaked in lukewarm
water for 15 minutes and
drained*
scant ¾ cup marmalade
*finely grated rind of 3
oranges*
¼ teaspoon ground cloves
1 teaspoon ground cinnamon

To make the pastry: sift the flour into a bowl, stir in the sugar, then make a well in the centre. Add the butter, 2 eggs, 1 egg yolk and the salt. Work the ingredients together with the fingertips to form a soft dough, then knead well until smooth and elastic. Shape the dough into a ball, cover and chill while making the filling.

Cook the figs in boiling water for 10 minutes. Drain thoroughly, then chop. Place in a bowl with the remaining filling ingredients and mix thoroughly.

Flatten the dough with a rolling pin and roll out to a sheet, about 5 mm/¼ inch thick. Cut into 10 cm/4 inch circles, using a pastry (cookie) cutter. Put a little filling in the middle of each circle, then fold the dough over the filling to form half-moon shapes. Moisten the edges with a little beaten egg white, then press firmly to seal.

Make a few cuts in the surface of each pasty and place on a greased baking (cookie) sheet. Brush with the remaining beaten egg to glaze. Bake in a preheated moderate oven (160°C/325°F/Gas Mark 3) for 25 to 30 minutes until puffed and golden. Serve hot or cold.

MAKES 6 TO 8

VECCHIARELLE

Honey-coated Fritters

Metric/Imperial	American
400 g/14 oz plain flour	*3½ cups all-purpose flour*
15 g/½ oz fresh yeast,	*½ cake compressed yeast,*
dissolved in 3 tablespoons	*dissolved in 3 tablespoons*
lukewarm water	*lukewarm water*
pinch of salt	*pinch of salt*
vegetable oil for deep-frying	*vegetable oil for deep-frying*
175 g/6 oz thin honey	*½ cup thin honey*

Sift the flour onto a work surface and make a well in the centre. Add the yeast and salt and work together with the fingertips. Add lukewarm water gradually, kneading until a smooth, pliable dough is obtained. Shape into a ball and place in a bowl. Sprinkle with a little flour and cover with a damp cloth. Leave to rise in a warm place for about 1 hour until doubled in bulk.

Knead the dough on a floured surface, then shape into small sticks, about 1 cm/½ inch thick and 6.5 cm/2½ inches long. Heat the oil in a deep-fryer and deep-fry the sticks, a few at a time, until golden brown. Drain on absorbent kitchen paper and keep warm while frying the remainder.

Put the honey in a saucepan and heat gently until it has melted, stirring constantly. Dip the sticks into the honey to coat and serve immediately.

SERVES 4 TO 6

PANINI DOLCI

Almond Yeast Cakes

Metric/Imperial	American
450 g/1 lb plain flour	*4 cups all-purpose flour*
pinch of salt	*pinch of salt*
pinch of ground cloves	*pinch of ground cloves*
pinch of ground cinnamon	*pinch of ground cinnamon*
50 g/2 oz blanched almonds,	*½ cup blanched almonds,*
toasted and chopped	*toasted and chopped*
200 g/7 oz caster sugar	*1 cup sugar*
1 teaspoon dried yeast,	*1 teaspoon active dry yeast,*
dissolved in 3–4	*dissolved in about ¼ cup*
tablespoons warm water	*warm water*

Sift the flour, salt and spices into a bowl and make a well in the centre. Add the remaining ingredients and work together with the fingertips. Add warm water gradually, mixing until a soft dough is obtained. Knead until smooth and elastic.

Form the dough into a ball, place in a bowl and cover with a damp cloth. Leave to rise in a warm place for 1 hour or until doubled in size.

Flatten the dough with a rolling pin and roll out to a sheet, about 1 cm/½ inch thick. Cut into small shapes, using different shaped pastry (cookie) cutters. Place on a greased and floured baking (cookie) sheet and bake in a preheated moderately hot oven (190°C/375°F/Gas Mark 5), for 15 minutes or until risen and golden brown. Transfer to a wire rack to cool before serving.

MAKES ABOUT 20

In 1533, when Catherine de Medici travelled from 'the court of Turin to France to be married to the Dauphin, she took her own pastry cooks with her. She feared the French pastry cooks would not be able to meet her high standards. Even today Italian housewives tend to leave pastry-making to the experts, seldom making pies and tarts at home. They prefer to buy them at their favourite pâtisserie, where they are bound to be spoilt for choice.

RICOTTA FRITTA

Ricotta Cheese Fritters

Metric/Imperial	American
50 g/1 lb fresh ricotta	*1 lb fresh ricotta cheese★*
cheese★	*all-purpose flour for coating*
plain flour for coating	*2 eggs, beaten*
eggs, beaten	*vegetable oil for deep-frying*
vegetable oil for deep-frying	*½ cup sugar*
90 g/4 oz caster sugar	

Cut the cheese into sticks, 4 cm/1½ inches long and 1 cm/½ inch across. Coat lightly with flour, taking care not to break them, then dip into the beaten eggs.

Heat the oil in a deep-fryer and deep-fry the ricotta slices, a few at a time, until golden brown. Drain on absorbent kitchen paper and keep warm while frying the remainder. Sprinkle with the sugar and serve immediately.

SERVES 4 TO 6

ZABAIONE

This most famous of all Italian desserts is very quick and simple to make, but make it immediately before serving as it is apt to separate if left to stand for more than a few minutes. A superb light dessert to complete a meal.

Metric/Imperial	American
4 egg yolks	4 egg yolks
4 tablespoons caster sugar	¼ cup sugar
1 tablespoon warm water	1 tablespoon warm water
7 tablespoons Marsala	7 tablespoons Marsala
sponge fingers to serve	lady fingers to serve

Place the egg yolks, sugar and warm water in a bowl over a saucepan of hot water. Beat with a balloon or rotary whisk (not an electric beater) until pale in colour and frothy.

Whisk in the Marsala a little at a time and continue whisking over heat for 5 to 10 minutes until the mixture increases in volume, becomes thick and foamy and holds its shape in a spoon.

Remove from the heat and spoon into tall wine glasses. Serve immediately with sponge fingers (lady fingers).

SERVES 3 TO 4

MANTECATO DI PESCHE

Peach Water Ice

A typical Sicilian fruit-based water ice. Melon ice can be made the same way, by replacing the peaches with 750 g/1½ lb ripe, peeled and deseeded ogen melon flesh

Metric/Imperial	American
100 g/4 oz sugar	½ cup sugar
150 ml/¼ pint water	⅔ cup water
4 large peaches	4 large peaches
juice of 1 lemon	juice of 1 lemon

Put the sugar and water into a small pan and heat gently until the sugar has dissolved, then boil for 3 to minutes. Leave until quite cold.

Immerse the peaches in boiling water for 1 minute then drain and remove the skins and stones (seeds Immediately, purée the flesh in an electric blender or press through a nylon sieve (strainer), then mix wit the lemon juice to prevent discolouration. Stir in th cold syrup, pour into a shallow freezer tray and freeze until half firm.

Turn into a bowl and whisk vigorously for a few minutes, then return to the tray and freeze until firm.

Transfer to the refrigerator 30 to 40 minutes befor serving to allow the ice to soften a little. To serve scoop the water ice into individual glasses.

SERVES 4

ABOVE: **Zabaione; Mantecato di pesche**

The Italians were the first Europeans to learn to make water ices and sherbets, but whether they learnt the art from the Arabs way back in the ninth century, or later from the Chinese during Marco Polo's time, is open to question. The Romans even had a rather crude form of water ice; it was a simple mixture of ice from the mountains with crushed fresh fruit.

SARDINIA

PÀRDULAS

Cream Cheesecakes

Metric/Imperial	American
PASTRY:	PASTRY:
400 g/14 oz plain flour	3½ cups all-purpose flour
pinch of salt	pinch of salt
100 g/4 oz lard, cut into pieces	½ cup shortening, cut into pieces
4–6 tablespoons water	4–6 tablespoons water
FILLING:	FILLING:
350 g/12 oz fresh cream cheese, sieved	1½ cups fresh cream cheese, sieved
175 g/6 oz caster sugar	¾ cup sugar
3 eggs, beaten	3 eggs, beaten
finely grated rind of 1 lemon	finely grated rind of 1 lemon
50 g/2 oz plain flour	½ cup all-purpose flour
pinch of saffron powder	pinch of saffron powder
pinch of ground cinnamon	pinch of ground cinnamon
pinch of salt	pinch of salt

To make the pastry: sift the flour and salt into a bowl and rub in the lard (shortening), using the fingertips. Mix in enough water to give a fairly stiff dough. Knead lightly until smooth. Cover and chill for 30 minutes.

Meanwhile, make the filling. Beat the cheese with the sugar, then gradually beat in the eggs. Add the lemon rind and sift in the flour with spices and salt. Stir well until thoroughly mixed.

Flatten the dough with a rolling pin and roll out to a thin sheet. Cut into circles about 10 cm/4 inches in diameter, using a pastry (cookie) cutter.

Put a little filling in the centre of each circle, then raise the edges of the dough around the filling and pinch them together with the fingertips to resemble tartlets with curly rims. Stand the pastries on a lightly oiled baking (cookie) sheet and bake in a preheated moderate oven (180°C/350°F/Gas Mark 4) for 30 minutes or until golden brown. Transfer to a wire rack to cool before serving.

MAKES 25 TO 30

Glossary

The most common terms used in Italian cooking, and the special ingredients which give the dishes their distinctive flavours (some are marked with a ★ in the recipes).

al dente   The term used to describe the perfect state of cooked pasta – soft and tender when bitten, but not sticky.

antipasto   Light starter or appetizer eaten before the main meal of the day. Antipasti is a selection of appetizers.

barolo   Robust red wine from the Piemonte region.

basil   One of the four most important herbs in Italian cooking. Freshly chopped, it is used on salads, pizzas and in sauces and soups. Combined with parmesan and pecorino, it makes pesto, the classic Genoese sauce for pasta.

bel paese   Mild-flavoured, soft, creamy cheese from Lombardy. Can be used as a substitute for mozzarella.

bitto   Another Lombardy cheese, made from cow's and goat's milk.

borage   Very popular in Italian cooking, the herb is used both as a flavouring and as a vegetable. In Genoa, the leaves are used as a stuffing for ravioli; they can also be served like spinach or dipped in batter and deep fried.

brodo   The Italian word for clear soup.

caciocavallo   Smooth Calabrian cheese with a spicy tang. Different shapes are coated in plastic and sold in pairs.

cannelloni   Large tubular shaped pasta usually stuffed with a variety of ingredients and baked in a sauce. Some do not have to be precooked.

capelletti   Round stuffed pasta shaped like little hats.

capelli d'angelo   Very fine pasta which resembles 'angel's hair' hence the name; usually sold coiled into nests.

cotechino   Spicy pork sausage from the Emilia-Romagna region.

dolcelatte   A type of gorgonzola.

finocchio   The name for Florence fennel, the bulbous vegetable much favoured in Italian cooking; whole, sliced or quartered it is braised or baked to serve as an accompaniment. It is also chopped and used raw in salads.

fontina   Rich creamy cheese from the Piemonte and Valle d'Aosta region. It is semi-hard, has a sweet nutty flavour and is used in rich dishes as well as eaten as a table cheese.

gorgonzola   Famous blue-veined cheese which takes its name from the town in Lombardy where it originated.

grana   The Italian word which describes any matured, hard cheese such as Parmesan which is grated and rarely eaten as a table cheese.

grissini   Thin, crisp bread sticks, originally from Turin, which are a feature of Italian eating.

maccheroni   Italian macaroni which is usually long like spaghetti, but much thicker and hollow. Short cut and elbow are other types of macaroni, as is rigatoni.

marsala   Famous fortified wine from Sicily used as a dessert wine, and in cooking.

mascarpone   A fresh cream cheese sold in muslin bags. Can be bought layered with gorgonzola to serve as a dessert cheese.

minestra, minestrone   Thick vegetable soups.

mozzarella   Originally made with buffalo's milk, but now more commonly made with cow's milk or a mixture of both. Eaten fresh when moist and dripping with whey, or cooked when dry. It is a good melting cheese and used in many Italian dishes.

origano   One of the four herbs essential to Italian cooking. Also known as wild marjoram, it grows all over the country and is used in pizzas, sauces and casseroles.

parmesan   Also known as *parmigiana*, this is perhaps the most famous of the *grana* cheeses. The most expensive ones have been matured longest (it takes at least two years to come to maturity).

pecorino   Hard cheese used for grating and cooking – it is quick maturing and therefore cheaper than parmesan.

pesto   Classic Genoese sauce for pasta.

polenta   Very popular in northern Italy as an accompaniment. It is made from maize flour and salted water – the coarser the flour, the more yellow the polenta.

prezzemolo   Italian flat-leafed parsley, sometimes called continental parsley. Has a stronger flavour than curly parsley and is used as a flavouring rather than a garnish.

primo piatto   The first course of a meal – usually soup.

prosciutto   Parma or San Daniele ham which is sold very finely sliced; cost is high because of the long ageing process needed to tenderize the meat.

provola, provolone   Oval plastic coated cheeses. *Provolone dolce* is young and mild; *provolone piccante* is mature and strong. In recipes calling for provola, use a mild *provolone*.

ragù   The famous meat sauce served with pasta – what the non-Italian calls spaghetti bolognese is really *ragù bolognese*.

ravioli   The general term for square or round filled pasta shapes served with butter and cheese, with a sauce or ragù, or in a clear soup.

ricotta   Soft white cheese with a crumbly texture and a mild bland flitoww £ which combines well with other ingredients, sweet or savoury. Curd or cottage cheese can be used as substitutes but the results won't be as good.

rigatoni   Ridged short macaroni.

salamelle, salsicchia a metro   Spicy, fresh pork sausages, the first sold in the conventional shape, the second in one long piece (hence a metro, by the metre). Some varieties are peppery hot.

scamorza   A type of mozzarella.

soppressata sausage   A speciality of the region of Apulia and Basilicata, the meat is coarsely cut rather than minced (ground) and then pressed. It is spicy with a high proportion of fat.

tortellini   Small rings of stuffed pasta served with butter, cheese or a meat or cream sauce.

vermicelli   Neapolitan name for spaghetti, the most common pasta outside Italy.

vernaccia   Sardinian dry white wine with a taste reminiscent of almonds.

zitone   Also called *zita* or *mezza zita*, this thick tubular pasta looks like extra large macaroni. *Zita* is thicker than *mezza zita*.

zuppa   Another word for soup, but usually reserved for those made with fish.

Index

ACKNOWLEDGMENTS

Special photography by Robert Golden – with the exception of 2–3 and 4–5, by Bryce Attwell
Food prepared by Caroline Ellwood
Photographic stylist: Antonia Gaunt

The publishers would also like to express their gratitude to the following companies for the loan of accessories for photography:

Sam Birrel; Craftsmen Potters Association, William Blake House, Marshall St, W1; Elizabeth David Ltd, 46 Bourne St, SW1; Divertiment Cooking and Tableware, 68 Marylebone Lane, W1; Kings Cross Continental Stores Ltd, 26 Caledonian Rd, N1; Pietro Negroni Ltd, Negroni House, 24 New Wharf Rd, N1; Figlio G. Parmigiani Ltd, 43 Frith St and 36A Old Compton St, W1; United Preservers Ltd, 8–10 Eldon Way, Abbey Rd, NW10; Vinorio, 8 Old Compton St, W1.

Essential Physical Science

ROCKS AND MINERALS

Chris Oxlade

Raintree is an imprint of Capstone Global Library Limited, a company incorporated in England and Wales having its registered office at 7 Pilgrim Street, London, EC4V 6LB – Registered company number: 6695582

To contact Raintree, please phone 0845 6044371, fax + 44 (0) 1865 312263, or email myorders@raintreepublishers.co.uk.

Text © Capstone Global Library Limited 2014

First published in hardback in 2014
The moral rights of the proprietor have been asserted.

Edited by Andrew Farrow and Abby Colich
Designed by Cynthia Akiyoshi
Original illustrations © Capstone Global Library Ltd 2014
Illustrated by HL Studios
Picture research by Tracy Cummins
Originated by Capstone Global Library Ltd
Printed in China by China Translation and Printing Services

ISBN 978-1-4062-5995-7
17 16 15 14 13
10 9 8 7 6 5 4 3 2 1

British Library Cataloguing in Publication Data
Oxlade, Chris.
  Rocks and minerals. -- (Essential physical science)
  1. Rocks--Juvenile literature. 2. Minerals--Juvenile literature.
  I. Title II. Series
  552-dc23
  ISBN-13: 9781406259957

Acknowledgements

We would like to thank the following for permission to reproduce photographs: Capstone Library: pp. 14 (Karon Dubke), 15 (Karon Dubke), 18 (Karon Dubke), 19 (Karon Dubke), 30 (Karon Dubke), 31 (Karon Dubke); Getty Images: pp. 13 (Carsten Peter/Speleoresearch & Films); 20 (Alan Majchrowicz), 21 (Ed Reschke), 25 (Dave Hamman), 28 (G. R. 'Dick' Roberts/NSIL), 32 (Ed Reschke), 35 (Jason Edwards); Photo Researches: pp. 10 (Phillip Hayson), 11 (Charles D. Winters / Science Source); Shutterstock: pp. 4 (© kojihirano), 5 (© scyther5), 7 (© PavelSvoboda), 9 (© beboy), 17 (© Qing Ding), 22 (© VLADJ55), 23 (© Ronald Sumners), 26 (© Katrina Brown), 27 (© berna namoglu), 37 (© Patryk Kosmider), 40 (© Offscreen), 41 (© Manamana), 42 (© John Copland); Superstock: pp. 16 (Brad Lewis / Science Faction), 29 (Universal Images Group), 34 (Louie Psihoyos / Science Faction), 36 (DeAgostini), 39 (PhotoAlto), 43 (Cubo Images).

Cover photographs of pebbles reproduced with permission from Superstock (Westend61).

Every effort has been made to contact copyright holders of material reproduced in this book. Any omissions will be rectified in subsequent printings if notice is given to the publisher.

Disclaimer

Contents

Eureka moment!

Learn about important discoveries that have brought about further knowledge and understanding.

DID YOU KNOW?

Discover fascinating facts about rocks and minerals.

WHAT'S NEXT?

Read about the latest research and advances in essential physical science.

Some words are shown in bold, **like this**. You can find out what they mean by looking in the glossary.

What are rocks and minerals?

You are never very far from a rock! Standing on the Earth's surface, there are usually rocks a few metres below your feet. Rocks form the surface of the Earth, and continue down into the Earth for many kilometres.

There are many different types of rock. You might have heard of some of them. How about sandstone, marble, or granite? If you haven't heard of them, you'll almost certainly have seen them. In many places, such a mountains and coasts, rocks are exposed at the Earth's surface. We also see them in homes and around town, as many buildings are constructed from rock. Materials such as **gravel** and sand are made up of particles of rock.

These amazing red, orange and white towers of sandstone rocks can be seen in the Bryce Canyon National Park in Utah, USA.

Minerals

Minerals are the materials that make up rocks. A mineral is a solid, non-living material. Most rocks are made up of a few different minerals mixed together. Quartz and feldspar are two of the most common minerals.

Rocks and minerals play an important role in our lives. As well as being a useful building material, rocks are a source of metals and precious stones such as diamonds. And we use minerals in many products, from **concrete** to toothpaste.

This ring is made from three materials found in rocks — the metal gold, and the precious stones diamonds and sapphires.

What's inside the Earth?

If you could dig a hole through the Earth you would discover that the rocks we see at the surface of the Earth only make up a thin **crust** on the outside of the Earth. All the rocks we talk about in this book are in the crust. Under the crust you would find very thick layers of rock before reaching the centre of the Earth.

Peeling the Earth

The main layers of the Earth are the crust, the mantle, and the core. Under the Earth's **continents** the crust is about 50 kilometres (30 miles) thick. There is also crust under the oceans, but here it is thinner – between 5 kilometres (3 miles) and 10 kilometres (6 miles) thick. The crust is very thin compared to the size of the Earth, which is 12,756 kilometres (7926 miles) across. You can think of it as being like the skin on an apple.

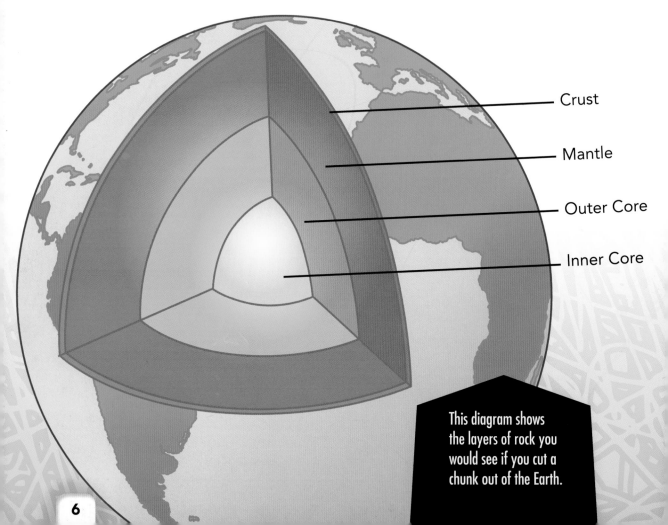

Crust

Mantle

Outer Core

Inner Core

This diagram shows the layers of rock you would see if you cut a chunk out of the Earth.

Under the crust is the mantle, which is the thickest layer of the Earth. Under the mantle, in the centre of the Earth, is the core. The rocks get hotter as you move towards the centre of the Earth. Right in the centre, the temperature is 4,700°C (8,500°F) or above.

DID YOU KNOW?

In some places on the Earth there are very hot rocks very close to the surface. This is often where there are volcanoes. A geyser is a spectacular natural fountain of boiling water caused by these rocks. When water flows down cracks into the rocks, it quickly boils, making steam. The steam blasts water back out of the cracks, making a fountain.

Tectonic plates

The crust (that's the thin, outer layer of the Earth) is broken into pieces called **tectonic plates**. Some are thousands of kilometres across, while others are just hundreds of kilometres across. Some plates are made up of thicker continental crust, some of thinner oceanic crust, and some of both sorts of crust.

The **tectonic plates** are moving, but very, very slowly. Even the quickest plates move at only about 10 cm (4 in) in a year, but over millions of years they move thousands of kilometres. Millions of years ago the continents were in different places from where they are today, and millions of years from now the continents will be in completely new positions.

This map shows the world's major tectonic plates. The jagged lines are where the plates are moving apart. The smooth lines are where they are colliding.

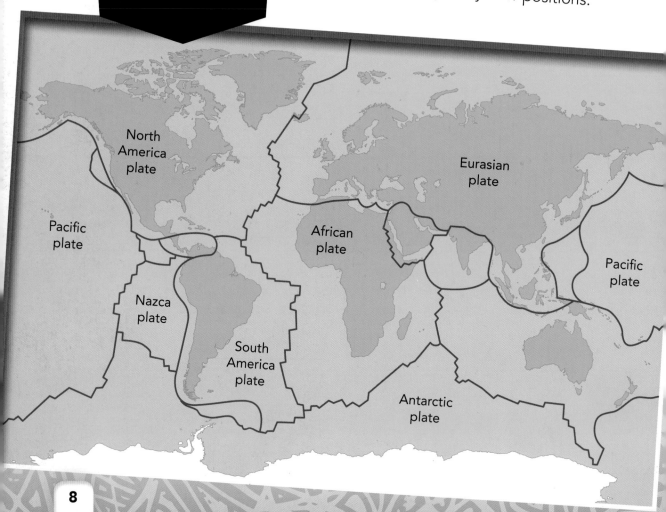

North America plate

Eurasian plate

Pacific plate

African plate

Pacific plate

Nazca plate

South America plate

Antarctic plate

At the edges

The places where one plate meets another are called **plate boundaries**. In some places the edges of the plates are moving apart. As they do, molten rock (called **magma**) rises from underneath the crust to fill the gap. In other places plates are moving towards each other. Their edges scrunch together and one plate slides down under the other. At these plate boundaries new rocks are formed and old rocks are changed.

Eureka!

Alfred Wegener (1880-1930) was a German scientist who realized that the coastlines of South America and Africa fit together like two pieces of a jigsaw. He suggested that the Earth's continents are slowly moving about. About 250 million years ago all the continents were joined together in one giant continent, which he called Pangaea.

Where tectonic plates move apart, molten rock sometimes reaches the surface, forming a volcano. When the lava cools, it forms new rock.

What minerals are there?

Minerals are made up of chemical **elements** joined together. For example, the mineral calcite is made up of the **elements** calcium, carbon, and oxygen, and the mineral quartz is made up of the elements silicon and oxygen. A few minerals are made up of just one element. For example, gold contains only the element gold, and diamond contains only carbon. Geologists divide minerals into groups depending on the elements they contain.

This is a close-up picture of a type of rock called granite. The light-coloured minerals are quartz and feldspar. The dark minerals are mica and hornblende.

Common minerals

There are thousands of different minerals in the Earth's rocks, but most rocks are made up of just a few minerals. The most common minerals found in rocks include feldspar, quartz, mica, and olivine. Feldspar is most common. It makes up about half of all rocks.

The properties of minerals

Geologists describe minerals by their properties. These properties include colour, lustre (whether they are dull or shiny), and transparency (how much light can shine through them). They also include hardness. This is tested using a scale called Moh's scale, which goes from 1 (very soft) to 10 (very hard). To find out the hardness of a mineral, the mineral is tested to see if it scratches a mineral of known hardness. Another important property is the shape of a mineral's **crystals** (see pages 12 and 13).

(see pages 12 and 13)

WHAT'S NEXT?

Geologists have discovered about 3,800 minerals in the Earth's crust. Each year they discover dozens more. Many minerals are useful for manufacturing things from concrete to electronic components. In the future we will probably find more minerals we can put to good use.

An assortment of minerals found in rocks, including silver, sulfur, sapphire, fluorite, ruby, galena, copper, beryl, malachite and azurite.

Crystals

Minerals are made up of particles, which are atoms or groups of atoms. In nearly all minerals the particles are arranged in neat three dimensional rows and columns, so they are neatly packed together. Materials with their particles arranged like this are called crystals.

One way that crystals form is when water that has minerals dissolved in it **evaporates**. As the water evaporates, the particles of the mineral join together, and a crystal begins to grow. Crystals grow with flat faces and straight edges. This is evidence that the particles are neatly arranged.

Mineral crystals also form when molten rock cools and turns to a solid. You can easily see these crystals in some types of rock, such as granite. The particles in mineral crystals are neatly arranged, but they don't have straight edges and flat faces you can see because each crystal is joined to the next.

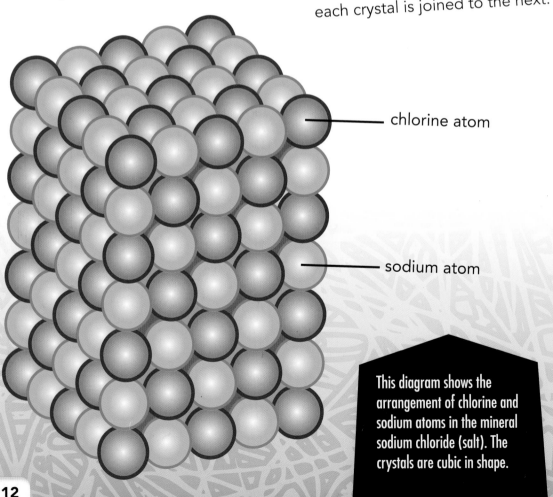

chlorine atom

sodium atom

This diagram shows the arrangement of chlorine and sodium atoms in the mineral sodium chloride (salt). The crystals are cubic in shape.

Crystal shapes

Different minerals have different shapes of crystals, with different numbers of faces and edges. Crystal shapes include cubic, which has six faces like a box, and hexagonal, which is like a cylinder with six faces around the outside.

Massive selenite crystals dwarf an explorer (dressed in orange in the back of the cave) in the amazing Cave of Crystals in northern Mexico.

Try this!

The minerals in rocks are normally in crystal form. Try this to grow your own crystals of the mineral magnesium sulfate (known as epsom salts).

Prediction

Crystals that grow freely (not in a confined space) will have straight edges and flat faces because their particles will join up in neat rows and columns.

Equipment

- epsom salts (You can obtain this from a pharmacist. An adult will have to buy it for you.)
- cup
- teaspoon
- dish
- magnifying glass

Ask an adult to help you with this experiment.

What you do

1. Boil some water in a kettle, then fill a cup with hot water.

2. Add a teaspoon of epsom salts to the water and stir to make the powder dissolve. Keep adding powder a teaspoon at a time until no more will dissolve in the water. You have made a solution of epsom salts.

3 Pour some of the solution into a dish, leaving behind any undissolved powder. Put the dish into the refrigerator.

4 Look at the dish every half an hour. After about an hour you should see many needle-like crystals have grown in the dish.

5 Pour away any remaining solution from the dish, and leave the crystals to dry.

6 Look closely at the crystals with a magnifying glass. Can you see the faces and edges of the crystals?

Results

Through a magnifying glass the crystals were seen to have flat faces and straight edges. This shows that their particles are neatly arranged.

What sorts of rock are there?

There are three types of rocks in the Earth's crust. They are **igneous rocks, sedimentary rocks,** and **metamorphic rocks.** The rocks are given these names because of the way they are made. There are many different rocks of each type.

Igneous rocks

Igneous rocks form when red-hot molten rock (called magma) cools down and becomes solid. Sometimes the magma comes out onto the Earth's surface, at volcanoes. At some volcanoes it comes out as runny rock, called lava. At other volcanoes the magma is blasted into tiny bits that fly high into the air and cool to make volcanic ash. Sometimes magma cools underground and turns solid, forming new igneous rock.

Lava flowing across Kamoamoa Black Sand Beach on the island of Hawaii. This sort of lava, which forms rounded mounds, is called pahoehoe lava.

Common igneous rocks

Basalt and granite are very common igneous rocks. Basalt is formed at volcanoes when lava cools quite quickly in the air. It is a black rock. Basalt is the most common rock in the Earth's crust. Granite is formed when magma cools slowly underground. It has grains large enough to see.

Recognizing igneous rocks

Examine a sample of rock through a magnifying glass. If you see crystals in different colours interlocked with each other, this normally means the rock is an igneous rock. Igneous rocks do not have flat or wavy layers of rock. They are also strong, and not crumbly like many sedimentary rocks.

DID YOU KNOW?

Pillow lava is a sort of igneous rock that forms when magma comes out of the sea bed, or flows into the sea from a volcano. The lava cools very quickly in the water and forms round lumps on top of each other.

This is the Giant's Causeway in Northern Ireland. The rock is basalt that split into six-sided columns as it cooled slowly underground.

Try This!

After runny magma comes out of a volcano's crater, it is called lava. Try this experiment with melted chocolate to see how lava flows and cools.

Prediction

When lava flows down the slopes of a volcano, it slows down as it cools and then goes solid. Also, when lava flows into water, it goes solid more quickly.

Equipment

- cooking chocolate or other plain chocolate
- baking tray
- large pan
- wooden spoon
- large glass bowl (slightly larger than pan so that it will rest inside the pan, but will not touch the bottom of the pan)
- oven glove

This experiment involves using a stove and handling hot pans. Ask an adult to help you.

Method

1 Break up your chocolate into small chunks and put them in a bowl.

2 Pour water into the pan until the water is a couple of inches deep, and put the pan on the stove.

3 Carefully put the bowl inside the pan (the bottom of the bowl must not touch the water), and begin heating the pan.

4 When the water is boiling, steam will come out around the edge of the bowl. Turn down the heat so that the water simmers gently. Stir the chocolate with a wooden spoon until it has all melted.

5 Lift the bowl with an oven glove and pour the chocolate onto one end of a baking tray.

6 Tip up the tray and watch the chocolate slowly flow along it.

7 You can model lava flowing into water, too. Prepare another bowl of water. Slowly pour some of the molten chocolate into the water and watch what happens.

Results

The flowing chocolate cools and slowly go hard, forming folds of chocolate. This is a model of how real lava flows and forms new igneous rock. When lava flows into water, the water cools it rapidly, and it goes solid very quickly.

Sedimentary rocks

Sediment is a material made up of millions of small bits of rock that have been deposited in water or by the wind. The sand on a beach is sediment, and so is the mud in an **estuary**. Sedimentary rock is rock that is made up of sediment, but with the pieces of rock joined to each other.

Sediment becomes solid rock when it gets buried under more and more layers of other sediments. Deep underground, under great pressure, the sediment gets squeezed, which makes the particles join together to make rock. This can take millions of years to happen.

Common sedimentary rocks

Common sedimentary rocks include sandstone, mudstone, and limestone. Sandstone is made when sand turns to rock, and mudstone is formed when mud turns to rock. There are several different types of limestone. Most limestones are made up of the skeletons or shells of tiny sea creatures, which fall to the seabed when the creatures die.

The cliffs on the Isle of Hoy in the Orkney Islands, Scotland, are made of red sandstone. You can see the different layers of sand in the rock.

Recognizing sedimentary rocks

You can often see the pieces of rock (the grains) that make up a piece of sedimentary rock. You might also be able to see layers of different sediments, made up of different-sized pieces of rock, or different-coloured pieces of rock. You might also be able to rub the grains off easily.

Eureka!

Englishman James Hutton (1726–97) was the first geologist to realize that sedimentary rocks are made when sediments are buried deep underground. He also realized that rocks on the surface of the Earth are broken down into the sediments that form new rocks.

This sedimentary rock is limestone. The rock is made up of the shells and skeletons of dead sea creatures.

Rocks from water

Some rocks form from minerals that are dissolved in water. As the water evaporates, or flows over existing rocks, the tiny particles of the minerals in the water join up to make new rock. All these rocks are types of limestone, which is made of a mineral called calcite. The calcite gets into the water when rainwater flows through limestone caves, and slowly dissolves the rock.

Metamorphic rocks

The word "metamorphic" means changing. Metamorphic rocks are made when sedimentary or igneous rocks are changed by pressure and heat deep underground in the Earth's crust. The pressure and heat make the minerals in the rock change into new minerals, and the crystals change size and shape. Common metamorphic rocks are gneiss, schist, marble, and slate.

This weird and wonderful limestone cave is in Croatia. The needle-like formations are called stalactites, which form as water drips form the cave roof.

Recognizing metamorphic rocks

In most metamorphic rocks, such as gneiss and schist, you can see bands of light and dark crystals. This pattern is called foliation. Some metamorphic rocks, such as quartzite and marble, are made up of crystals of just one mineral.

Meteorites

A **meteorite** is a lump of rock not from the Earth but from space. Millions of bits of rock from space hurtle into the Earth's **atmosphere**. But some reach the surface, and these are meteorites. They are bits of rock left over from when the **solar system** was made, or that were thrown into space by collisions between planets and moons.

WHAT'S NEXT?

Astronomers are interested in the rocks that make up the other rocky planets and moons in the solar system. These rocks can tell us about how the solar system formed. **Space probes** to other planets analyze the rocks they find and send data back to Earth. In 2012 the Mars Science Laboratory landed on Mars, carrying instruments to analyze the Martian rocks.

The Leaning Tower of Pisa, in Italy, is constructed from beautiful white marble, which is a metamorphic rock. Much of the world's marble comes from Italy.

How do rocks change?

The surface of the Earth seems like a very solid place to us. But all the time, new rocks are being made, and old rocks are being worn away or turned into different types of rock. Most of these changes take place over millions of years. As the rocks change, the surface of the Earth changes too. For example, new mountains are built up and worn away.

Making new rocks

New igneous rocks are made where magma cools, at volcanoes on the Earth's surface, under the ground, and under the sea. New sedimentary rocks are made underground and under the seabed as layers of sediments are squeezed together.

This is a diagram of how the three types of rock are formed and change into each other. This called the **rock cycle.**

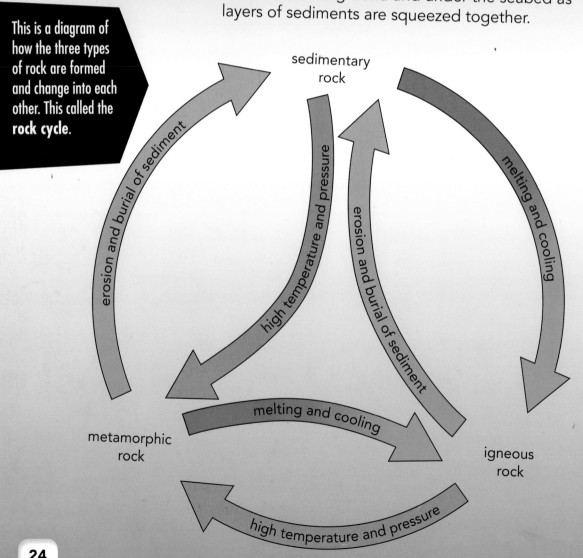

sedimentary rock

erosion and burial of sediment

high temperature and pressure

erosion and burial of sediment

melting and cooling

metamorphic rock

melting and cooling

igneous rock

high temperature and pressure

Destroying rocks

Rocks are broken down by **erosion** (see page 26), which wear away the rocks at the Earth's surface and in caves under the ground. Rocks are always destroyed at some plate boundaries, where rocks at the edges of plates are pushed down into the mantle and melt.

Changing rocks

Sedimentary rocks and igneous rocks are changed into metamorphic rocks, and metamorphic rocks are changed into different metamorphic rocks. These changes happen at plate boundaries, where rocks are squeezed by huge forces, and where the heat of red-hot magma changes the rocks.

Eureka!

Under the world's oceans there is a mountain chain a total of 80,000 kilometres (50,000 miles) long. It's called the Mid-Ocean Ridge system. In 1953, two American geologists, Maurice Ewing and Bruce Heezen, discovered a deep canyon running along the ridge. This showed where tectonic plates are moving apart, and where magma rises to make new rock.

The light-coloured mud has been made by erosion of rocks, washed down a river, and deposited here, in the Okavango Delta, Botswana. It may go on to become new sedimentary rock.

Weathering

The weather is one thing that destroys rocks. The hot Sun heats rock in the day, the rock expands slightly, then at night the rock cools and contracts. This gradually weakens the rock, and eventually pieces fall off. Freezing weather also breaks up rock. If water trickles into cracks in rocks, then freezes to make ice, the ice expands and widens the crack. Eventually the rock breaks apart. We call these processes **weathering**. Piles of broken rocks at the bottom of mountains (called scree) are often made by weathering.

The rocky towers of Monument Valley in Utah, USA, are the remains of a sheet of rock that has been destroyed by weathering and erosion.

Erosion

Erosion is how moving water, the wind, and **glaciers** destroy rocks. Flowing water knocks pieces off rocks as it flows over them. This happens in rivers and at coasts as waves hit the shore. Pieces of rock moved by the water help to smash pieces off the rocks. This is how rivers cut deep river valleys, and how the sea breaks up the seashore. Sand blown along by the wind also erodes rocks, as the particles of sand knock bits off rock they hit. Then the wind blows the bits away. Glaciers gouge (scrape) at rock as they flow slowly down mountains, and carry the rock away.

The bits of rock made by erosion form sediments that might go on to form new sedimentary rock, and also become soils (see pages 28–29).

Pebbles are chunks of rock that have rounded and smoothed by being rubbed and bashed against each other by the power of waves hitting the shore.

DID YOU KNOW?

Chemical weathering happens when rainwater flows over rocks. The water is slightly acidic because it contains dissolved carbon dioxide, and so it dissolves the rock. Limestone dissolves more quickly than other rocks, and chemical weathering creates amazing caves, passages, and weird rock shapes in limestone, which dissolves in water.

Soil

Much of the Earth's landscape is covered with a layer of soil. In some places the soil is just a few millimetres thick; in others it's many metres deep. Underneath the soil is the top layer of rocks in the crust, known as bedrock. Soil is a mixture of bits of rock and material from plants that have rotted, which is called humus, as well as water and air.

Soil is made by weathering and erosion. Millions of small bits of rock made by weathering and erosion form sediments. Then plants take root in the sediments, and micro-organisms and other animals move in.

DID YOU KNOW?

Just one kilogram of soil (that's about a cupful) contains an amazing number of micro-organisms. There may be around 500 billion bacteria, a billion fungi, and 500 million tiny animals.

In this photograph, you can see layers of soil close to a river in New Zealand. The top, dark layer contains living matter such as roots and micro-organisms, and dead plant matter.

Living in the soil

Soil is teeming with life. Most organisms in the soil are micro-organisms such as bacteria and fungi. These feed on dead plant matter, such as leaves that fall to the ground. Worms, insects, and millipedes also live in the soil. They help to mix the soil and get air into it, which helps plants to grow.

Soils for growing

Soils contain chemicals called nutrients, which plants need in order to grow properly. Nutrients come from rotting plant matter and from rocks. The best soils for growing crops are found alongside rivers and around volcanoes. When rivers flood they bring new sediments, and so new nutrients to the land next to the rivers. Volcanic soils are made from weathered and eroded volcanic rocks.

Valuable soil has been eroded away in this part of Mexico because the trees that hold the soil together have been cut down.

Try this!

Flowing water erodes rock. It also moves sediments from one place to another. Sediments can go on to form sedimentary rocks. Try this experiment to see the power of water at work.

Prediction

When water flows over sediments, it picks up particles and moves them along. When the water slows down, the sediments are left behind.

Equipment

- some play sand
- two old medium-sized shallow trays (plastic trays or baking trays)
- old cup
- some newspaper
- small plastic box (a few centimetres high)

Method

1. Cover your working surface with newspaper to protect it in case you spill sand and water.

2. Put two cupfuls of sand onto a tray and spread it out evenly.

3 Put another tray on your work surface, and position the tray with sand so that one corner is over one end of the lower tray. Prop up the opposite corner with a small box so that the tray slopes down from this corner.

4 Fill a cup with water. Now slowly pour water into the upper corner of the sand-filled tray. Water should flow across the upper tray and into the lower tray.

5 Watch what happens to the sand in the lower tray.

Results
The sand in the upper tray is eroded and then deposited on the lower tray. This shows that flowing water moves sediment from one place to another.

What are fossils?

Fossils are the imprints of ancient animals and plants that are found in rocks. They are formed when the remains are trapped in sediments and the sediments are turned to rock. Fossils tell us about life on Earth in the distant past.

Forming fossils

Most fossils form when plants or animals are buried quickly by sediments after they die. Normally only the hard parts of animals and plants, such as bones, shells, and woody stems, become fossils. But sometimes the softer parts, such as leaves and feathers leave a pattern in the sediment before they rot. Animal footprints are sometimes fossilized too. Most fossils are found in limestone and shale. Some sedimentary rocks, such as shelly limestone and chalk are made up completely of fossils of sea creatures.

A beautiful fossil of part of a fern, which died and was buried in a swamp 270 to 300 million years ago.

Coal

Coal is known as a fossil fuel because it formed over millions of years from the remains of plants. The plants lived in ancient swampy forests, and started to rot as they died. Then they were buried under sediments. Over millions of years underground the water was squeezed out of them, and they turned into coal.

WHAT'S NEXT?

Fossils of animals and plants that lived millions of years ago are helping scientists to discover more about climate change. The types of animals and plants that lived in different parts of the world are clues to what the climate was like then. They help us to build a picture of how the Earth's climate changed in the past, and how it might change in the future.

Animal dies and is quickly covered with sediment.

Soft parts of animal (skin, muscle, etc.) rot away, leaving skeleton.

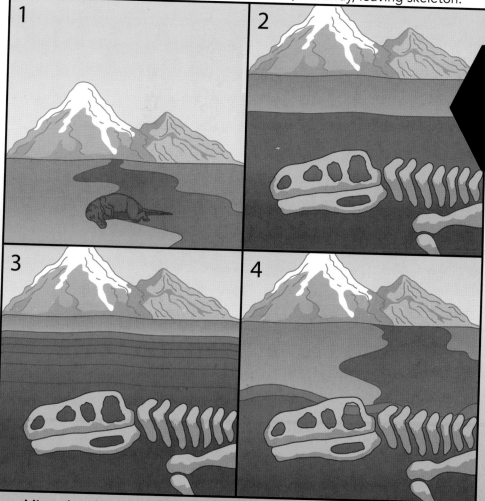

This diagram shows the stages in the formation of a dinosaur fossil.

Minerals in bone change as rock forms.

After millions of years rock is eroded and fossil exposed at surface.

Finding fossils

Fossils appear on the Earth's surface when the layers of sedimentary rocks they are buried under are eroded away. They might have been buried for millions, or even hundreds of millions of years. When rare fossils are found, paleontologists dig them out with great care. Sometimes fossilized bones can be put together to see what the skeletons of ancient animals looked like.

Paleontologist Luis Chiappe is digging the skull of a protoceratops (a type of plant-eating dinosaur) from the rocks of the Gobi desert in Asia.

DID YOU KNOW?

Fossils are clues to events that happened on Earth millions of years ago. We have found thousands of dinosaur fossils that are more than 65 million years old, but none that is less that 65 million years old. Scientists think that much of life on Earth, including all the dinosaurs, was wiped out when a huge meteorite hit the Earth.

What fossils tell us

Nearly everything we know about life on Earth in the distant past comes from fossils. We know about the different animals and plants, and when they lived. And we know when different animals began living on the Earth, and when they died out. Without fossils, we wouldn't know that animals such as the dinosaurs ever lived.

Eureka!

In 1861, fossils of a chicken-sized animal with feathers were discovered in the region of Bavaria in Germany. The fossils are about 150 million years old. The new animal was given the name Archaeopteryx. It has some of the features of a bird, and some of the features of a dinosaur. It may have been the very first type of bird.

A rare fossil of Archaeopteryx, which is thought to be the earliest type of bird. You can see the shape of the feathers attached to the skeleton.

How do we use rocks?

Rock is an important material because of its properties. We use hard rocks for making things, from houses to ornaments, and soft rock such as clay for making pottery. We get all the metals we need from rocks, and many useful minerals, too.

These ancient cutting tools were made tens of millions of years ago by chipping away at pieces of flint. They were found in Austria.

Early rock tools

Rock was one of the first materials that humans used, along with wood and animal skins and bones. Flint was the most useful sort of rock. Archaeologists have found flint tools that people used tens of thousands of years ago for cutting up the animals they hunted and for shaping wood. This period in history is known as the Stone Age.

Rock for building

Rocks are used all over the world as a building material. The best building rock is rock that is easy to cut and shape, but that doesn't crumble and stands up to weathering. Clay is a very soft rock that goes very hard when it is heated in a kiln. It is moulded into shape to make bricks and tiles. Concrete is made from rock, too. It contains **cement**, which is made from limestone, and gravel or crushed rock. Road surfaces are also made from crushed rock.

WHAT'S NEXT?

Some of the other planets in the solar system, their moons, and **asteroids** are all made of rock. These rocks may contain minerals that don't exist on Earth, and elements that are very rare on Earth. Mining companies are making plans to send robots to these other worlds to find and bring back these materials.

Buildings such as this mill in Ireland are often made of locally available rock cut into blocks and cemented together. Here the roof is made of clay tiles.

Metals from rocks

Most of the metals we use today come from rock in the Earth's crust. They include iron (which is used to make steel), aluminium, and copper. These are all chemical elements, and they are all contained in minerals found in rocks. The minerals we get metals from are called metal ores. For example, the main ore from which we get aluminium is called bauxite, and the main ore of iron is haematite. The first stage in producing metals is to dig the ores out of the ground, in mines and quarries, and sometimes by dredging them from the seabed.

DID YOU KNOW?

Small chunks of gold called nuggets are found in some sediments of gravel and sand. They can be found using a method called panning. The gravel is swirled around in a shallow pan so that gold, which is heavier than the rock pieces, falls to bottom.

Getting metals out

Different methods are used to get metals from their ores. For example, to get aluminium from bauxite, the bauxite is molten and then electricity is passed through it. This removes the aluminium. To get iron from haematite, the haematite is heated and the oxygen is removed to leave molten iron. This process is called smelting.

Native metals

A few metals are found in rocks as elements. They are not part of minerals. They include gold, silver, and platinum. This is why gold was one of first metals to be discovered, thousands of years ago.

Eureka!

Ten thousand years ago, the only materials people knew how to use were wood, stone, and animal skins and bones. Metals were discovered one by one by accident. First was copper, discovered about 5000 BC. Later, copper was mixed with tin to make bronze. Iron was discovered by about 500 BC.

Iron comes from iron ore. The ore is heated with carbon in a blast furnace. This releases the iron from the ore, and molten iron is poured out.

Rock for decoration

Rocks are cut into slabs and polished smooth to give a beautiful finish. They are used as decorative stone on the floors and walls of buildings, and for worktops and table tops in kitchens. As well as being attractive to look at, they are strong and long-lasting. Sculptors cut and shape rock to make sculptures, and practical objects such as vases and containers.

Marble can be cut and carved into intricate shapes such as the top of this column.

Marble

Marble is a very popular decorative stone, especially for floor tiles and wall tiles, and for sculpture. Marble is limestone that has been changed by heat and pressure deep underground. It comes in a huge variety of colours and patterns. The finest and most expensive marble comes from Italy.

Gemstones

Rubies, emeralds, sapphires, and diamonds are examples of gemstones. They are minerals found in rocks that are beautiful because of their colour, but are also very rare, and very hard-wearing. Their main use is in jewellery, when they are cut and polished. Some have other uses, such as diamonds for drills and rubies for lasers. Other gemstones are more common. Examples are agate, a mineral that contains beautiful rings of colour, jasper, and amethyst.

This bright green mineral is garnet uvarovite. The crystals are too small to be used for gemstones, but pieces can be polished to make decorative stones.

What have we learned about rocks?

**Rocks are the materials that make up the
Earth's crust – the outer layer of the Earth.
Minerals are materials that rocks are made of.**

There are three types of rock, which are sedimentary rocks,
igneous rocks, and metamorphic rocks. Sedimentary rocks
are made up of layers of sediments, such as sand and mud,
that have been buried deep underground. Igneous rocks are
made when molten rock cools. Metamorphic rocks are made
when rocks are changed by immense heat and pressure.
Rocks are always being made, changed and destroyed. This
is known as the rock cycle.

There are spectacular rock
formations all over the world.
This is Sugar Loaf Mountain in Rio
de Janeiro, Brazil, which is the
solid core of an extinct volcano.

Rocks tell us about the animals and plants that lived on Earth long before because they contain fossils. In fact, we only know that they existed because of fossils.

Rocks and minerals are useful materials. We use rocks as building materials, get the metals we need from minerals, and use fossil fuels for power. We couldn't live our modern lives without rocks. We depend on them like the people who lived in the Stone Age, tens of thousands of years ago.

WHAT'S NEXT?

Now you know a little about rocks and minerals, you could start your own rock, mineral and fossil collection. Perhaps you could collect pebbles from a stony beach, where you might find many different types of rocks. Make a note of where and when you found the rocks. Never take rocks from sensitive areas such as nature reserves, or important geological sites. You can often find mineral specimens for sale.

Museums often have collections of interesting rocks and minerals, such as these strange fluorescent minerals.

Glossary

asteroid large piece of rock smaller than a planet that orbits the Sun

astronomer scientist who studies space and the objects in space

atmosphere the layer of air that surrounds the Earth

cement material made with lime from limestone and clay, used to make mortar and concrete

concrete construction material that is made with cement, water, sand and gravel

continent large body of land on the Earth's surface (there are seven continents)

crust the solid outer layer of the Earth, which is made of solid rock

crystal material in which the particles are arranged in neat rows and columns, so they are neatly packed together

element substance made of atoms that cannot be broken down into simpler substances

erosion wearing away of a surface by the weather, flowing water, waves, and so on

estuary the lowest section of a river, where the river meets the sea

evaporate to change from a liquid to a gas

fossil remains of an ancient plant or animal found in rock

geologist scientist who studies the rocks of the Earth's crust

glacier body of ice that flows slowly downhill, like a river of ice

gravel material made up of numerous small stones, which can be rounded or jagged

igneous rock rock formed when molten rock (magma or lava) cools and goes solid

magma molten rock under or in the Earth's crust

metamorphic rock type of rock formed when rocks are changed by heat and pressure, normally deep underground

meteorite piece of rock from space that enters the Earth's atmosphere and hits the Earth's surface

mineral one of many solid, non-living materials that makes up rocks

plate boundary line along which two tectonic plates meet

rock cycle process in which new rocks are continuously made and old rocks are continuously destroyed or changed in new rocks

sediment material made from numerous small pieces of rock, or numerous shells or skeletons of sea creatures

sedimentary rock type of rock formed from layers of sediment (which may be particles of rock or the shells or skeletons of sea creatures)

solar system the Sun, the planets and their moons, and other material that orbits the Sun

space probe spacecraft sent from Earth to visit other objects (such as planets or moons) in the solar system

tectonic plate one of the many large pieces that the Earth's crust is cracked into

volcano place where magma comes out onto the Earth's surface, or a mountain formed from solidified lava and ash

weathering breaking down of rock by the action of the weather (such as hot and cold, or ice)

Find out more

Books

DK Pocket Eyewitness Rocks and Minerals (Dorling Kindersley, 2012)

Investigating Rocks (Do It Yourself series), Will Hurd (Heinemann Library, 2010)

Let's Rock series (Igneous Rocks, Sedimentary Rocks, Metamorphic Rocks, Fossils, Minerals, Soil, Crystals) (Raintree, 2012)

Spotter's Guides: Rocks and Minerals, Alan Woolley (Usborne Publishing, 2007)

Websites

http://mineralsciences.si.edu/
This site explores the Mineral Sciences section of the website of the Smithsonian Institute in the United States.

http://www.nhm.ac.uk/nature-online/earth/rock-minerals/
This is the rocks and minerals page of London's Natural History Museum, including a huge database of rocks, minerals and fossils found in the UK.

http://www.oum.ox.ac.uk/thezone/index.htm
Oxford University Museum of Natural History's Learning Zone has fun things to do on the subject of rocks, fossils, and minerals.

Further research

There's lots more to find out about rocks and minerals. Here are some ideas for further research:

• What rocks make up the landscape where you live? You can often find the answers to this in your local museum, which may have a geological display.

• Where are rocks and minerals used around your home, and in your area? Look at utensils and ornaments in your home and garden, and at other local buildings. Can you identify any of the rocks and minerals? A simple field guide to rocks and minerals will help.

Index